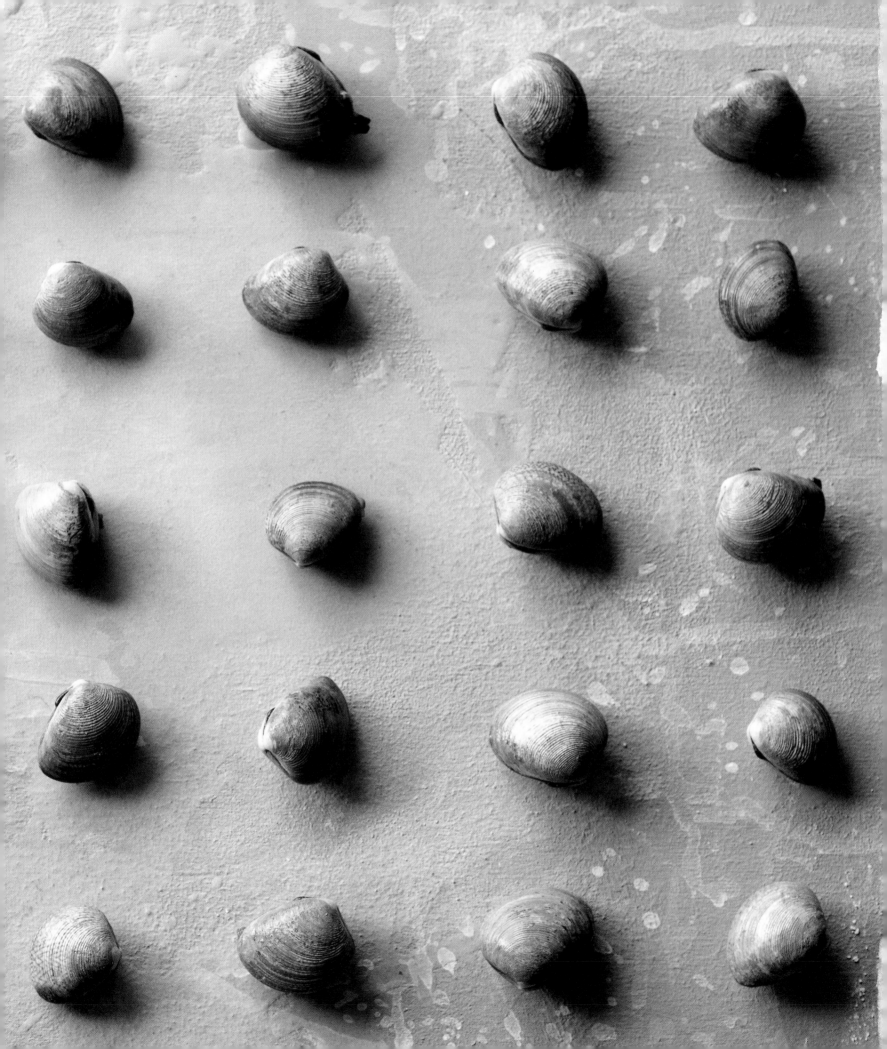

This book is dedicated to my father, Angus Muir (1927-1995), who liked to throw a line in, enjoyed a good meal, loved to read and taught me to strive to be the best I can be.

SYDNEY SEAFOOD SCHOOL COOKBOOK

ROBERTA MUIR

PHOTOGRAPHY BY ALAN BENSON

LANTERN
an imprint of
PENGUIN BOOKS

CONTENTS

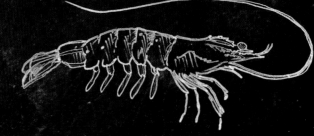

INTRODUCTION

Sydney Seafood School was opened in November 1989, when Australia's obsession with food was in its infancy. What we now call 'Modern Australian' cuisine was just emerging, French cooking dominated the restaurant guides, and Asian ingredients that are widely available today (such as lemongrass, kaffir lime and fish sauce) were still considered exotic.

The New South Wales fishing fleet caught plenty of whiting, snapper and flathead to supply the local market, and, in doing so, they also netted octopus, red mullet, leatherjacket, crabs and other species that most home cooks didn't know how to prepare. A large part of the catch was sold as bait — or for next to nothing to those who did appreciate it — so the School was established to teach people how to cook some of the more unusual species and help create a demand for the huge variety of seafood found in our oceans.

Over the years, Sydney Seafood School has grown to become Australia's largest cooking school. Australians have become such adventurous eaters that mussels, octopus and crabs are now commonly cooked at home, and abalone, sea urchin and sashimi are widely enjoyed. Around 13,000 people attend classes every year, and leading chefs from Sydney and interstate share their expertise in a wide range of cuisines and cooking styles. All of the recipes in this book have been taught at the School over its 23-year history.

Australian waters are rich with an incredible diversity of seafood species, which can be broadly divided into two categories: finfish (commonly just called 'fish') and shellfish (which can be further subdivided into univalves, bivalves, cephalopods and crustaceans). This book has been organised along these lines, as many similar species are interchangeable in recipes; we've given some alternative suggestions with most recipes too. Sauces and accompaniments can also be mixed and matched between recipes or served with a plain piece of pan-fried or steamed fish — so feel free to experiment.

Medical experts are increasingly encouraging us to eat more seafood. It is relatively low in fat and cholesterol and high in essential nutrients, including omega-3 oils, protein, vitamins and minerals, making it an important part of a healthy diet.

There is, however, increasing concern about the sustainability of the world's seafood. The good news is that, while overfishing has been a serious problem globally and continues to be an issue in some regions, since the turn of this century Australian fisheries have been internationally recognised as among the best-managed in the world. Our stocks of even previously overfished species continue to increase under careful supervision.

One of the best things we can do to maintain a healthy, sustainable diet is to eat as wide a variety of food as possible. Hopefully, the recipes in this book will encourage you to try some different seafood species and other ingredients, and to try your hand at new ways of preparing them.

Almost all of Australia's leading chefs have taught at the Seafood School; there's nothing they seem to enjoy more than talking about food and sharing their passion with like-minded people. Over the 15 years I've run the School, I've attended hundreds of classes — you'd think I'd be an expert by now, but I still learn something new at every class. Throughout the book, you'll find advice about choosing, storing and cooking seafood, as well as helpful tips in the recipe introductions. With a little guidance, seafood is one of the easiest foods to cook — so dive in and enjoy!

RECIPE GUIDE

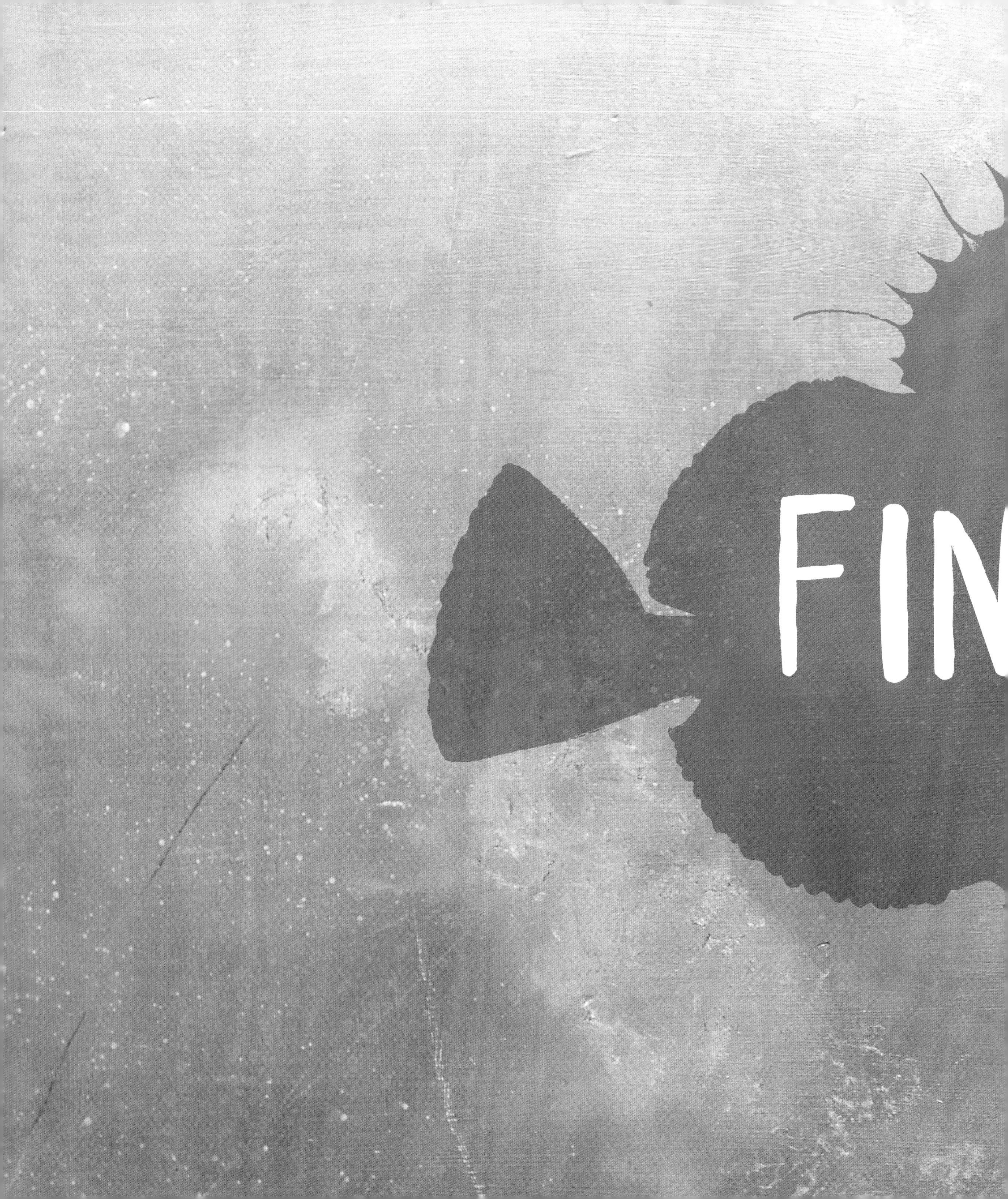
FIN

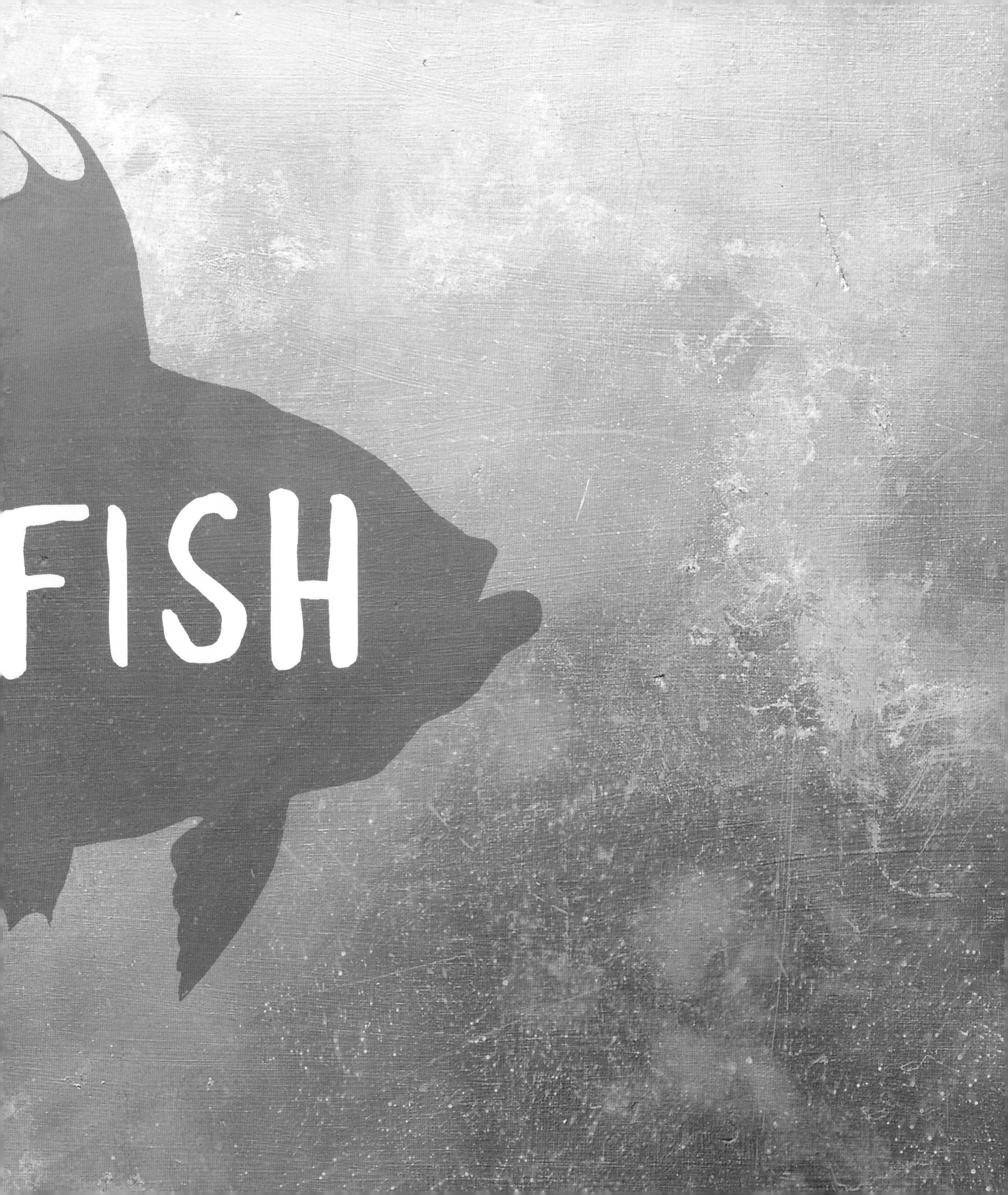
FISH

SILVER PERCH

BARRAMUNDI

FRESHWATER FISH

RAINBOW TROUT

MURRAY COD

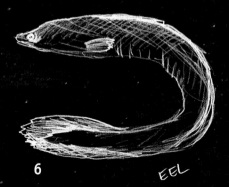

EEL

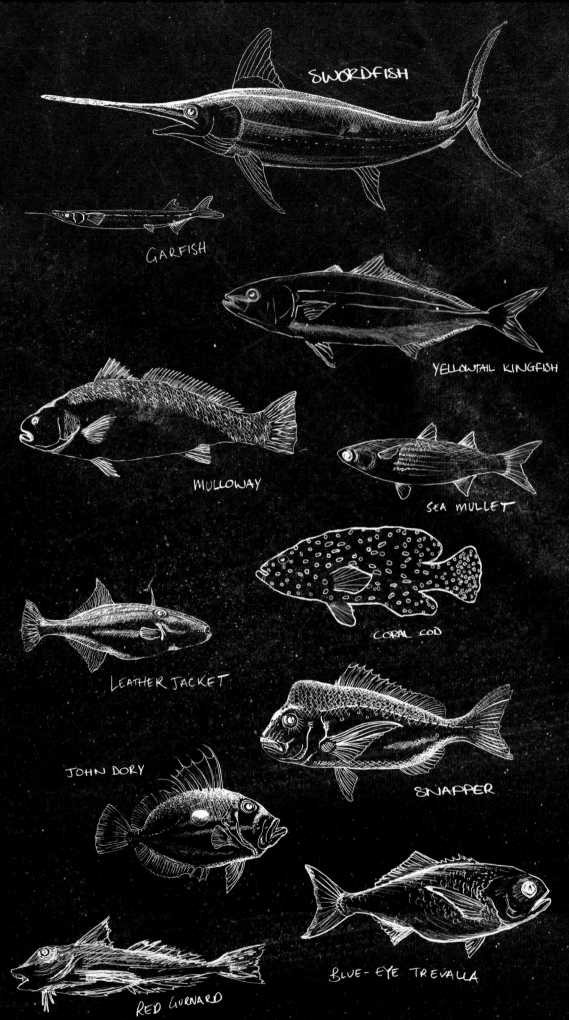

SWORDFISH

GARFISH

YELLOWTAIL KINGFISH

MULLOWAY

SEA MULLET

CORAL COD

LEATHER JACKET

JOHN DORY

SNAPPER

RED GURNARD

BLUE-EYE TREVALLA

6

OCEAN TROUT

AUSTRALIAN SARDINE

BLUE MACKEREL

YELLOWFIN TUNA

ATLANTIC SALMON

KING GEORGE WHITING

SILVER TREVALLY

YELLOWFIN BREAM

CORAL TROUT

FinFish

GOLDBAND SNAPPER

HAPUKU

BAR ROCK COD

RED EMPEROR

BASS GROPER

FLATHEAD

RED MULLET

EASTERN RED SCORPIONFISH

SKATE

CHOOSING & STORING FINFISH

WHOLE TRUNK FILLET BUTTERFLIED PIECES OF FILLET STEAKS CUTLETS

Australians are lucky to have such a diverse array of fish and shellfish, making it unnecessary to eat frozen, imported seafood. Develop a rapport with your fishmonger and ask about what fish is freshest and best on the day. If what you want isn't available, choose from the list of alternative species suggested with each recipe, or ask the fishmonger for a suitable replacement. If possible, buy fish whole and ask your fishmonger to fillet it for you, rather than buying fillets (save the bones for fish stock).

Fish are sold in several forms:

* **whole:** usually with the gills, guts and scales removed;
* **trunk:** the same as whole but with the head, and sometimes skin, removed;
* **fillet:** the whole side of a fish cut away from the central backbone and rib cage;
* **butterflied:** both fillets joined along the back by skin, with the bones removed (mostly used for small fish, such as sardines);
* **pieces of fillet:** large fillets cut into serving-sized portions;
* **steaks:** very large fish, such as swordfish or tuna, cut into four boneless loins, then sliced into steaks;
* **cutlets:** sections sliced widthways through the whole fish, leaving the bones in.

The eggs, or roe, of some fish are also commonly eaten. Sturgeon roe (caviar) is perhaps the best known. Considered a delicacy, it is produced from farmed fish in various countries including France and the USA. Salmon roe is produced in Australia; the large orange eggs add colour and texture to dishes. Bottarga is the pressed, dried roe sac of grey mullet; it looks like a flattened orange sausage and is served sliced or grated. Tobiko, flying fish roe, is imported from Asia; these tiny little eggs add crunch and colour and are sometimes sold flavoured with ginger, chilli or wasabi. 'White roe' is also sometimes available from fishmongers; it has a delicate custard-like texture and flavour.

 When choosing whole fish, look for:

* bright and lustrous skin and scales;
* firm flesh that springs back when touched;
* bright pink–red gills (if they haven't been removed);
* a pleasant fresh sea smell.

Clear eyes are sometimes mentioned as a sign of freshness, but as eyes can turn cloudy if they come into contact with ice, this isn't always a reliable indicator.

When choosing fillets, steaks and cutlets, look for:

* bright, lustrous and firm flesh (any dark muscle should be a pink–red colour);
* no discolouration, gaping or bruising;
* a pleasant fresh sea smell.

 Freshness is important with any food, but with seafood it's paramount. Fish will stay fresh for longer if they're kept cold. When shopping, use a chiller bag or esky, and ask your fishmonger to pack some ice with your purchase.

When you get home, scale, clean and gut the fish if necessary (fishmongers will usually do this for you). If you need to clean the fish, wipe it with a damp cloth – do not rinse it under running water, as you'll wash away a lot of flavour. To store, place the fish on a plate or tray, or in a lidded container. Cover with a damp cloth, then plastic wrap or the lid. Store in the coldest part of the fridge and use within 2–3 days. It's always preferable to buy seafood just before you intend to eat it. However, if you want to freeze fish, you should scale, gut and clean them, then place them in an airtight freezer bag, extracting as much air as possible. Whole non-oily fish can be frozen for up to 6 months at -18°C or less, while whole oily fish and all fish fillets, steaks and cutlets can be frozen for up to 3 months at -18°C or less.

Before cooking fillets, trim off the thinner ends and the belly flaps to create a uniform thickness for even cooking. Trimmings can be used for fish cakes or soups (or fed to the cat!).

PREPARING FINFISH

SCALING

1 Holding the fish by the tail, place it inside a plastic bag. Run the back of a butter knife (or a fish scaler) along the skin to dislodge the scales.

2 Remove the fish from the bag and wipe any remaining scales off with a clean, damp cloth.

SCALING FISH CAN BE VERY MESSY AS THE STICKY SCALES FLY EVERYWHERE. THIS METHOD USING A PLASTIC BAG MAKES IT MUCH EASIER TO CLEAN UP AFTERWARDS.

FILLETING

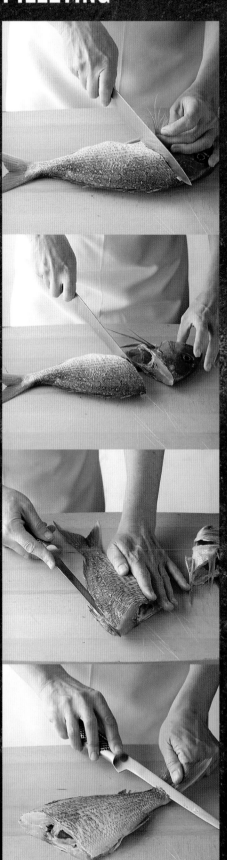

1 Lift up the side fin and, using a cook's knife, cut at an angle just below the head.

2 Remove the head and the flap containing the lower front fins.

3 Using a filleting knife (see Seafood kit), make an incision along the top of the fish from the head end to the tail.

4 Holding the tail, make an incision into the flesh at the base of the tail.

5 Starting from the tail and placing the other hand gently on the fish to keep it steady, run the knife flat along the backbone to separate the fillet from the bone.

6 When nearing the head end, hold the tail to keep the fish in place and finish cutting all the way through to separate the fillet from the bone.

7 Lift off the fillet. Turn the fish over and repeat on the other side, starting with Step 3.

8 Cut out and discard rib bones from both fillets (see Step 8 on page 13).

SKINNING

1   Place the fillet on a chopping board, skin-side down. Use a pinch of salt on your fingers to help grip the tail. Using a filleting knife (see Seafood kit), make an incision into the flesh at the tail end.

2   Holding the knife firmly and keeping it parallel to the board, pull the tail back and forth so that the blade slides between the flesh and the skin.

PIN-BONING

1   Run your finger along the centre of the fillet to find the bones. Place a finger on either side of the bone to prevent the flesh tearing. Grasp the bone with fish tweezers (see Seafood kit) and pull towards the head end (the same direction as the bone runs). Dip the tweezers in water to dislodge the bone, then repeat with the remaining bones.

2   Alternatively, cut along either side of the bones and discard this section. Called a 'V-cut', this is a suitable method when the fish has a dark central bloodline that you also want to discard.

BUTTERFLYING SMALL FISH
This method is for butterflying fish that are already gutted.

1

Lift up the side fin and, using a filleting knife (see Seafood kit), cut at an angle to remove the head and the flap containing the lower front fins.

2

Using kitchen scissors, trim off the top and bottom fins.

3

Make an incision along the belly of the fish from the head end to the tail. Wipe out the belly with a clean, damp cloth, if necessary.

4

Open the fish out and place it on a chopping board, flesh-side down. Gently press the heel of your hand along the back of the fish to loosen the backbone.

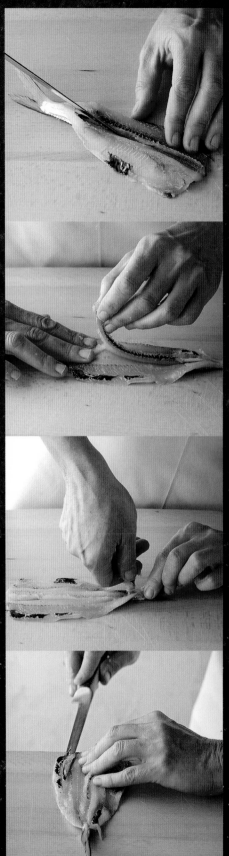

5

Turn the fish over so that it is skin-side down. Run the tip of the knife at a 45-degree angle along either side of the backbone.

6

Grasp the backbone at the head end and, holding the flesh in place with the other hand to prevent it tearing, pull the backbone up and away from the fish.

7

When you reach the tail, bend the backbone back and twist it off.

8

Turn the fish 90 degrees. Run the knife just underneath the rib bones on one side, a few at a time, to remove them. Turn the fish 180 degrees and repeat with the rib bones on the other side.

ASSEMBLING

'Cooking' seafood can be as easy as assembling some raw, seared, cured or smoked fish with other top-quality ingredients. Chefs are increasingly serving seafood raw, as sashimi, crudo or tartare, or just very lightly seared. It's easy to create a simple yet impressive dish with sashimi-grade fish and just a handful of other ingredients. Seared fish is a great introduction for people who love fish but aren't quite sure about eating it raw.

Seafood has such a delicate structure that it can be 'cooked' by coming into contact with an acidic marinade, such as lemon or lime juice. Ceviche, seafood marinated in citrus juice and eaten without further cooking, is a classic dish from Central and South America.

Cured or smoked fish is a perfect base for a quick, substantial salad or smart entrée. Fish was traditionally cured by soaking it in brine or rubbing it with salt, often with other flavourings added. Before modern cold-storage, canning and easy transportation, seafood was often cured to extend its shelf-life, but these days it's cured for variety and flavour.

Smoking was another early form of food preservation. Today, seafood is only lightly smoked to add flavour. There are two basic methods of smoking: cold-smoking, in which fish is surrounded with smoke so that the flavour penetrates the flesh, but at such a low temperature (usually below 26°C) that it remains raw, such as with cold-smoked salmon; and hot-smoking, in which fish is initially cold-smoked, then the temperature is raised and the fish is cooked in the smoky environment, for example smoked whole rainbow trout.

TIPS FOR SUCCESSFUL ASSEMBLING

* **Use only sashimi-grade seafood if serving it raw or rare.** 'Sashimi-grade' means the seafood is suitable for eating raw; it's caught and handled in such a way that peak freshness and quality are maintained. Fish are line-caught, landed onto a mattress (to minimise bruising) and killed instantly by brain-spiking (the Japanese term *ike jime* is sometimes used for this procedure). This prevents the fish from struggling and releasing stress hormones and helps to keep the body temperature low. The fish is then bled immediately, removing heat and waste products, and put into an ice-slurry to drop the body temperature as close to 0°C as quickly as possible

* **Freshness is paramount.** Keep raw seafood well chilled and consume it on the day of purchase. After more than 24 hours in a domestic fridge, sashimi-grade fish will still be premium quality but it won't be at peak freshness. Cook any leftovers – don't serve them raw the following day.

* **Observe good hygiene.** Wash your hands before starting to prepare the seafood and before and after handling other ingredients. Clean utensils, knives and boards between ingredients to avoid cross-contamination.

* **Remove seafood from the fridge 15–30 minutes before serving.** Flavour can be dulled by low temperatures.

Recipe by
Guillaume Brahimi

YELLOWTAIL KINGFISH SERVED TRADITIONALLY

SERVES 6 AS AN ENTRÉE

3 eggs, hard-boiled, yolks and whites separated

900 g piece sashimi-grade yellowtail kingfish, skin off, pin-boned and trimmed of any bloodline

3 tablespoons crème fraîche

juice of 1 lemon, strained

½ bunch chives, finely snipped

salt flakes and freshly ground white pepper, to taste

3 teaspoons salmon or ocean trout roe

ALTERNATIVE SPECIES:
snapper

This dish draws its inspiration from a classic way of serving caviar, with sieved eggs, soured cream and chives. At Guillaume at Bennelong, Guillaume Brahimi uses Sterling caviar, from white sturgeon farmed in the USA. Orange pearls of salmon or trout roe are a more affordable alternative for home entertaining, but feel free to splash out on caviar if the mood takes you.

Pass the egg yolks and whites separately through a fine sieve.

Slice the fish into strips about 5 mm thick. Combine the crème fraîche and lemon juice and spread 2 teaspoons on each plate. Lay the fish over the top, then sprinkle with egg yolk, egg white, chives, salt and pepper. Top each serving with ½ teaspoon of roe.

CRUDO OF LEATHERJACKET

Recipe by
Tetsuya Wakuda

Leatherjacket is related to Japan's highly prized fugu fish, but comes without the risk of poisoning. Tetsuya Wakuda presented this recipe in a Seafood School class in 1997, saying that when he first arrived in Australia and tasted leatherjacket, he loved it because it was so similar to fugu in taste and texture, but all the Australians he knew said, 'Mate, you don't eat that, it's bait!'. Many people still haven't realised what a wonderful fish leatherjacket is, which means it's always a bargain.

This recipe makes more ponzu dressing than is needed, but the excess can be stored in an airtight container in the fridge for a few days and is great as a salad dressing. Ponzu is a Japanese citrus-based sauce (don't use ponzu shoyu, ponzu mixed with soy sauce, for this dish). It and shiro dashi (a Japanese liquid stock-base) are available from Asian grocery stores; if shiro dashi is unavailable, use the same amount of instant dashi granules.

Slice the fish as thinly as possible on an angle of about 20 degrees, so that each slice is a couple of centimetres wide. Place on a serving plate.

To make the ponzu dressing, whisk all the ingredients together.

Spoon a small amount of the dressing over the fish. Mound the daikon on top and serve.

SERVES 6 AS AN APPETISER

1 × 150 g sashimi-grade leatherjacket fillet, skin off and pin-boned

1 tablespoon finely grated daikon (white radish), squeezed to remove excess moisture

Ponzu dressing

2½ tablespoons ponzu

25 ml soy sauce

2½ teaspoons mirin

2 teaspoons caster sugar

¾ teaspoon shiro dashi

1 tablespoon extra virgin olive oil

ALTERNATIVE SPECIES:
john dory; snapper

Recipe by
Dan Hong

BRUSCHETTA OF RAW SILVER TREVALLY WITH SHISO, PRESERVED LEMON & MISO RANCH DRESSING

SERVES 6 AS AN ENTRÉE

1 sourdough baguette

extra virgin olive oil, for drizzling

600 g sashimi-grade silver trevally fillets, skin off and pin-boned

8 purple shiso leaves, roughly sliced

½ bunch coriander, leaves picked and torn

1 stalk celery heart, thinly sliced

1 preserved lemon, rind rinsed and finely chopped

1 bunch chives, finely snipped

salt flakes, to taste

55 g salmon or ocean trout roe

Miso ranch dressing

100 g sour cream

100 g Japanese mayonnaise

2 tablespoons milk

40 g white miso paste

2 tablespoons strained lemon juice

¾ tablespoon onion powder

1 teaspoon garlic powder

ALTERNATIVE SPECIES:
snapper; tuna; yellowtail kingfish; saucer scallop

Dan Hong is part of the TOYS (Taste of Young Sydney) collective, a group of Sydney's brightest young restaurant talent keen to prove what the next generation is capable of. While they come from varied culinary backgrounds, one of their trademarks is making food fun, and they like to play around with giving fast food a gourmet edge – as with Dan's take on America's popular ranch dressing in this dish.

Preheat the oven to 190°C (fan-forced).

To make the miso ranch dressing, whisk all the ingredients together until smooth and well combined. Refrigerate until needed.

Cut the baguette on an angle into 1 cm-thick slices about 8 cm long, and place on a paper-lined baking tray in a single layer. Drizzle with oil and cook for 7–8 minutes, until golden and crisp but still a bit chewy in the centre.

Slice the fish into fine strips, discarding any bloodline. Place in a mixing bowl with the shiso, coriander, celery heart, preserved lemon rind, chives, salt and miso ranch dressing. Using a spoon, mix to combine well.

Divide the fish mixture among the baguette croûtons and garnish with roe.

Recipe by
Mark Best

TONNATO TONNATO

SERVES 6 AS AN ENTRÉE

1 × 800 g piece sashimi-grade yellowfin tuna loin, skin off and trimmed of any bloodline

200 g salted butter

1 fresh bay leaf

2 sprigs thyme

2 cloves garlic, crushed

salt flakes and freshly ground black pepper, to taste

200 g fine fresh breadcrumbs (see Chefs' ingredients)

vegetable oil, for deep-frying

1 bunch curly parsley, picked into small sprigs

50 g anchovy fillets in olive oil (see Chefs' ingredients), halved lengthways, oil reserved for Tonnato sauce

Tonnato sauce

250 g preserved tuna in olive oil (see Chefs' ingredients), drained, oil reserved

2 egg yolks

60 g brined capers, drained

25 ml white wine vinegar (see Chefs' ingredients)

200 ml extra virgin olive oil

salt flakes and freshly ground black pepper, to taste

ALTERNATIVE SPECIES:
albacore; bonito; Spanish mackerel

Vitello tonnato is a classic Italian dish of thinly sliced poached veal covered in a tuna mayonnaise. The name means 'veal in the style of tuna', as the veal is poached, then left covered in the tuna mayonnaise for a day or more until it has the soft, flaky texture of cooked tuna and has absorbed some of its flavour. It takes a mind like Mark Best's to come up with this delicious version that is literally 'tuna in the style of tuna'. You can roll the tuna and prepare the sauce the day before and refrigerate both overnight, ready to just slice and serve the following day.

Remove any remaining skin or bloodline from the tuna.

Take four sheets of plastic wrap long enough to wrap around the tuna loin at least twice, and lay them on top of each other. Place the fish at one end and roll up the plastic wrap as tightly as possible. Twist the ends to seal tightly, then refrigerate for at least 3 hours, 4–5 hours if possible, or overnight.

To make the tonnato sauce, place the drained tuna in a food processor with the egg yolks, capers, vinegar and the oil reserved from the anchovies. Blend until smooth, then, with the motor running, slowly add the oil reserved from the tuna. With the motor still running, slowly add the olive oil. Blend in a good grind of pepper, then taste and add more salt or pepper if needed. If necessary, add a tablespoon or two of hot water to achieve the consistency of thickened cream. Set the tonnato sauce aside, covered, at room temperature (or refrigerate if serving the next day).

About half an hour before serving, place the butter, bay leaf, thyme, garlic and a good grind of pepper in a frying pan and heat until the butter is foaming. Add the breadcrumbs and stir over medium heat until golden. Add salt. Cover the pan to keep the breadcrumbs warm until needed.

Preheat the vegetable oil to 170°C (see page 61). Add the parsley sprigs and fry for a few seconds until they stop popping, then remove them with a slotted spoon. Drain on paper towel, and cover with more paper towel to keep warm until needed.

Using a very sharp knife, slice the tuna through the plastic wrap into thin slices. Divide the tonnato sauce among plates, spreading it out into a circle, and arrange the tuna slices on top, discarding the plastic wrap. Add a grind of pepper and garnish with the breadcrumbs, parsley sprigs and anchovy strips.

Recipe by
Alessandro Pavoni

OCEAN TROUT CRUDO WITH CUTTLEFISH INK MAYONNAISE & CRISP MANDARIN

1 × 600 g piece sashimi-grade ocean trout fillet (1.5–2 cm thick), skin on and pin-boned

2 tablespoons Mandarin dressing (see below)

1 tablespoon Cuttlefish ink mayonnaise (see below)

1½ tablespoons salmon or ocean trout roe

½ punnet baby lemon balm (see Chefs' ingredients), snipped

5 g freeze-dried mandarin

½ sheet nori, halved lengthways and sliced into fine strips

salt flakes, to taste

Curing mixture

1 tablespoon caster sugar

⅔ cup (80 g) salt flakes

finely grated zest of 1 lemon

¼ bunch dill, leaves finely chopped

Mandarin dressing

½ cup (125 ml) strained freshly squeezed mandarin juice

1 teaspoon caster sugar

1½ teaspoons salt flakes

100 ml extra virgin olive oil

Cuttlefish ink mayonnaise

1 egg yolk

3 teaspoons cuttlefish ink

1 teaspoon salt flakes

1 teaspoon strained lemon juice

1 teaspoon white wine vinegar (see Chefs' ingredients)

100 ml grapeseed oil

ALTERNATIVE SPECIES:
salmon

Alessandro Pavoni is passionate about authentic regional Italian cooking, but he also loves to experiment with exciting new techniques, textures and flavour combinations. This pretty dish is one of his more avant garde combinations, using freeze-dried fruit (made by New Zealand company Fresh As and available from specialist food shops and online). The dressing and mayonnaise recipes both make more than you'll need for this dish, but it's hard to blend smaller quantities; they'll keep in the fridge for a few days and are delicious on salads or grilled seafood. Cuttlefish ink is available in small sachets and jars from some fishmongers and delis. It's often referred to as 'squid ink', but is in fact ink from cuttlefish.

To make the curing mixture, combine all the ingredients.

Rub the curing mixture all over the flesh side of the fish, then cover it in plastic wrap and refrigerate it for 45 minutes.

Meanwhile, to make the mandarin dressing, combine the mandarin juice, sugar and salt in a blender. With the motor running, slowly drizzle in the oil to create an emulsion. Set aside.

To make the cuttlefish ink mayonnaise, combine the egg yolk, cuttlefish ink, salt, lemon juice and vinegar in a food processor. With the motor running, slowly drizzle in the oil to create an emulsion. Set aside.

Wipe the curing mixture off the fish with a clean, damp cloth. Remove the skin and halve the fish lengthways, discarding any bloodline. Slice the fish on an angle, as finely as possible. Divide the fish slices among six shallow bowls, laying them out in a slightly overlapping single layer.

To serve, drizzle over the mandarin dressing and add some dots of cuttlefish ink mayonnaise. Decorate with roe, lemon balm and freeze-dried mandarin. Scatter the nori over the top and sprinkle with salt.

CURED SALMON WITH EXTRA VIRGIN OLIVE OIL & GOLDEN SHALLOTS

Recipe by
Tony Bilson

Tony Bilson presented this elegant recipe at a workshop he taught at the Seafood School in its early days, back in 1997, which goes to show that good food never dates! You'll need to start this recipe a day or two ahead to give the fish time to cure and marinate. Once cured, the fish will keep, completely covered in the oil, for up to a week in the fridge.

Blanch the shallot slices in boiling water for 1 minute. Drain in a sieve, then run under cold water and press to extract excess liquid.

Combine the shallot, pepper and oil in a bowl, then cover with plastic wrap and refrigerate for 24 hours.

Meanwhile, to make the curing mixture, combine all the ingredients. Place three pieces of foil, each one and a half times as long as the salmon fillet, on top of each other and make a bed for the fish using a third of the curing mixture. Place the fish on top, skin-side down, and cover with the remaining two thirds of the curing mixture. Fold the foil over the fish and seal with a double fold. Place in a baking dish and refrigerate for 12–24 hours – but no longer or the fish will start to dry out and become tough.

Unwrap the fish and wipe off the curing mixture with a clean, damp cloth. Place the fish in a clean non-reactive baking dish and pour the oil and shallot mixture over it. Cover with plastic wrap and refrigerate for 12–24 hours.

Remove the fish from the dish, scraping any shallots off the fish and back into the oil. Transfer the oil and shallot mixture to a small serving bowl.

Cut the fish into very thin slices on an angle, leaving the skin behind, and arrange on a cold serving plate. Spoon a little oil and shallot mixture over the fish and garnish with chervil sprigs and pepper. Serve the remaining oil and shallot mixture on the side.

SERVES 12 AS AN ENTRÉE

6 golden shallots, sliced

freshly ground black pepper, to taste

200 ml extra virgin olive oil

1 × 1.5–2 kg sashimi-grade salmon fillet, skin on and pin-boned

chervil sprigs, for garnishing

Curing mixture

1 cup (220 g) caster sugar

1 cup (120 g) salt flakes

2 tablespoons thyme leaves

1 tablespoon freshly ground white pepper

ALTERNATIVE SPECIES:
ocean trout; snapper

BACCALA MANTECATO
ALLA VENEZIANA

Recipe by
James Kidman

This classic Venetian dish is one of the most delicious ways to prepare baccala, salted cod imported from Europe. When he was head chef at Otto, James Kidman demonstrated this recipe at Gusto, the Italian festival held at the Seafood School each year, and we lived off the delicious leftovers for the next week! It is very moreish – slightly salty, fluffy and great to share from a big bowl with pre-dinner drinks. Baccala is available from some delis and fishmongers (don't buy stockfish, which has been air-dried and is much harder). If you buy salt cod on the bone, you'll need about 1.5 kg. Start this recipe a day ahead: it's important to soak the cod well to extract most of the salt.

Soak the salt cod, covered, in the fridge for 24–36 hours, changing the water every few hours when possible (but at least three times).

The next day, drain the cod and place it in a large saucepan of water. Bring to the boil, then reduce the heat and simmer for about 10 minutes, until cooked through. Remove the cod from the water and, when cool enough to handle, break the flesh into small pieces, discarding any skin, bones and dark bits.

Place the oil in a small saucepan and heat it to about 70°C (see page 61); the oil should be hot but not sizzling. Cover with a lid and set aside to keep warm.

Combine the milk, cream, garlic, bay leaf and thyme in a saucepan. Bring to the boil, then remove from the heat. Discard the bay leaf and thyme. Remove the garlic, then cover the pan to keep warm. Place the garlic in a mortar and pound with a pestle to form a paste.

Place the cod and the garlic paste in the bowl of an upright electric mixer fitted with a whisk. While beating on medium–high speed, slowly and carefully add a little of the hot milk mixture, then a little hot oil, alternating until all the milk mixture and oil has been added and regularly scraping down the sides of the bowl. Beat for a further minute or two on high speed, until it sounds like the paste is slapping against the sides of the bowl.

Transfer to a serving bowl and serve warm with olives and grilled bread.

SERVES 6 AS AN ENTRÉE

1.1 kg salt cod fillets (baccala), skin on

325 ml extra virgin olive oil

150 ml milk

150 ml pouring cream

3 cloves garlic, peeled

1 fresh bay leaf

3 sprigs thyme

Ligurian olives, for serving

grilled sourdough bread, for serving

ALTERNATIVE SPECIES:
none

Recipe by
Philippe Mouchel

SALMON RILLETTES

SERVES 6 AS AN ENTRÉE

1 × 150 g piece salmon fillet,
skin off and pin-boned

100 ml extra virgin olive oil

salt flakes and freshly ground
white pepper, to taste

12 thin slices brioche

100 g smoked salmon, diced

1 teaspoon strained lemon juice

1 teaspoon chopped dill

1 teaspoon pouring cream

2 tablespoons salmon or ocean trout roe

12 chervil leaves

ALTERNATIVE SPECIES:
*blue mackerel (replacing the smoked salmon
with extra blue mackerel); ocean trout;
rainbow trout*

Rillettes are generally made with pork, or occasionally duck or rabbit. The cooked meat is mixed with fat, shredded into thin, moist strands and served with crisp croûtons. French chef Philippe Mouchel, who has run restaurants in both Sydney and Melbourne, presented a seafood spin on this classic dish at the Seafood School. You can prepare these rillettes a day in advance, making them perfect for a dinner-party entrée or an accompaniment to pre-dinner drinks. If brioche is unavailable, use thin slices of baguette or other firm white bread drizzled with olive oil.

Preheat the oven to 130°C (fan-forced). Brush the salmon with a little of the oil, then sprinkle it with salt and pepper and place it on a baking tray. Place the brioche on a separate baking tray. Place both trays in the oven for 10–15 minutes, until the salmon fillet is cooked through. Remove the salmon from the oven, then increase the oven temperature to 180°C (fan-forced) and continue cooking the brioche until crisp and golden. Set the salmon and brioche aside to cool.

Flake the cooled salmon into small pieces and place in a mixing bowl. Add the smoked salmon, lemon juice, dill, cream, salt, pepper and remaining oil and mix together until well combined. Gently stir through the roe. Refrigerate, preferably overnight, until you are ready to serve.

Garnish the rillettes with chervil and serve with the brioche croûtons.

Recipe by
Stefano Manfredi

SALAD OF HOT-SMOKED RAINBOW TROUT, TREVISO & GREEN BEANS

SERVES 8 AS AN ENTRÉE

600 g young green beans, trimmed

1 clove garlic, minced

1 handful flat-leaf parsley leaves, finely chopped

salt flakes and freshly ground black pepper, to taste

⅔ cup (160 ml) extra virgin olive oil

1 tablespoon wholegrain mustard

⅔ cup (160 ml) red wine vinegar (see Chefs' ingredients)

2 hot-smoked rainbow trout, skin and bones removed and flesh broken into bite-sized pieces

1 treviso radicchio, trimmed and thinly sliced

ALTERNATIVE SPECIES:
hot-smoked brook trout or any other freshwater trout

In landlocked parts of northern Italy such as Lombardy, where Stefano Manfredi was born, freshwater fish from the many rivers and lakes are popular. In Australia, most of our seafood is saltwater (due to our abundant coastline) but freshwater rainbow trout is widely available, especially in hot-smoked form. In this hearty salad, the trout combines deliciously with treviso, a type of radicchio originally from northern Italy. The only cooking required is boiling the beans.

Blanch the beans in plenty of rapidly boiling salted water for a couple of minutes, until they are tender but still have some bite.

Meanwhile, combine the garlic, parsley, salt, pepper and half the oil in a large bowl.

Drain the beans well, then add them to the bowl and toss to coat.

Whisk together the mustard, vinegar and remaining oil to make a dressing.

Toss the trout with the treviso, beans and dressing. Serve immediately, piling some of the trout on top of the salad.

Recipe by
Warren Turnbull

SMOKED EEL PÂTÉ, PICKLED CUCUMBER & SPRING ONION FLATBREAD

1 × 500 g smoked eel

finely grated zest and strained juice
of 1 lemon

1 teaspoon Spanish unsmoked hot paprika
(see Chefs' ingredients)

400 g sour cream

2 tablespoons freshly grated horseradish

2 eggs, hard-boiled and roughly chopped

1 tablespoon chopped dill

flatbread, for serving (see Basics)

Pickled cucumber

1 telegraph (long) cucumber, peeled,
halved and sliced into thick chunks

salt flakes, to taste

3 tablespoons Japanese rice vinegar

60 g caster sugar

1 stem dill, leaves picked and
finely chopped

Spring onion salsa

1 bunch spring onions (scallions),
green and white parts, roughly chopped

½ bunch mint, stalks and leaves torn

½ bunch flat-leaf parsley, stalks
and leaves torn

2 cloves garlic, roughly chopped

salt flakes and freshly ground
white pepper, to taste

about 3 tablespoons extra virgin olive oil

ALTERNATIVE SPECIES:
*hot-smoked salmon, trout or
any other hot-smoked fish*

Fresh eels can be a bit tricky to tackle as they're usually sold live, but smoked eel is a breeze to prepare and it's delicious! At District Dining, where this dish is often on the menu, Warren Turnbull makes his own flatbread, but you can use a ready-to-bake pizza base from the supermarket if you prefer. The pâté tastes even better if it's made a few hours in advance, so it's perfect for entertaining.

To make the pickled cucumber, sprinkle the cucumber with salt and set aside in a small bowl at room temperature. Heat the vinegar, sugar and ½ cup (125 ml) of water in a small saucepan over medium heat until the sugar dissolves. Remove the pan from the heat and set it aside to cool. When cool, pour the mixture over the salted cucumber and set it aside for 10–15 minutes. Drain the cucumber in a colander, place in a bowl and toss with dill. Refrigerate until needed.

Remove the eel's head and cut fillets from either side of the backbone. Using a teaspoon, scrape the remaining meat from the backbone. Peel off the skin and check for any fine bones. Place the eel meat, lemon zest, paprika, sour cream and horseradish in a food processor and process until a paste forms. Spoon the paste into a bowl and fold through the lemon juice, egg and dill. Refrigerate the pâté until you are ready to serve, removing it from the fridge 15–30 minutes before serving.

To make the spring onion salsa, place the spring onion, mint, parsley, garlic, salt and pepper in a food processor and blitz until combined. With the motor running, drizzle in enough oil to make a coarse paste.

Spread the flatbread with the spring onion salsa and arrange on a platter with the smoked eel pâté and the pickled cucumber.

BAKING

Baking is a great way to prepare large whole fish, which may be too big for a frying pan but will fit on a baking tray. It's also an excellent way to heat shellfish gently without overcooking them. And of course all sorts of seafood pies and tarts wouldn't be possible without ovens.

Some dishes combine baking with other cooking methods. What the Italians call *al cartoccio* and the French call *en papillote* involves wrapping fish in a paper parcel and cooking it in the oven so that it steams in its own juices. Braising and baking can also be combined by putting seafood in a covered baking dish with some liquid. Chefs also often combine baking or roasting and pan-frying, searing a fillet in a frying pan for colour, then finishing it off in the gentler heat of the oven.

TIPS FOR SUCCESSFUL BAKING

❋ **Remove seafood from the fridge 15–30 minutes before cooking** to allow it to come to room temperature. This is particularly important if fish is whole, quite thick or being served rare.

❋ **Score whole fish before baking.** Cut through the thickest part of the flesh to the bone at intervals on both sides – this allows even heat penetration.

❋ **Baste the fish occasionally to keep it moist.**

❋ **Take the fish out of the oven just before it's fully cooked.** It will continue to cook in the residual heat once it's removed from the oven.

❋ **Rest the cooked fish for 5–10 minutes.** When you remove the whole fish or large pieces of fillet from the oven, cover and set the fish aside in a warm place for 5–10 minutes (depending on thickness); this gives time for the juices that have been drawn to the surface by the heat of cooking to seep back towards the centre, ensuring the fish will be moist throughout.

Recipe by
Justin North

MACKEREL TARTE FINE

SERVES 6 AS AN ENTRÉE

200 g butter puff pastry
(see Chefs' ingredients)

2 large vine-ripened tomatoes,
quartered and thinly sliced

12 anchovy fillets in oil, drained and halved
lengthways (see Chefs' ingredients)

12 picholine or other green olives,
cheeks cut from the pit

finely grated zest of 1 lemon

extra virgin olive oil, for drizzling

3 × 100 g blue mackerel fillets, skin on

Basil oil

1 bunch basil, leaves picked

1 clove garlic, peeled

juice of 1 lemon, strained

salt flakes and freshly ground
white pepper, to taste

200 ml extra virgin olive oil

ALTERNATIVE SPECIES:
*Australian sardine; bonito; hot-smoked trout;
tuna*

While Justin North's dishes at Bécasse are often quite complex creations, he also likes to show that French food can be light and simple. *Tarte fine* is the simplest of French tarts, a thin puff-pastry base covered with a sweet or savoury topping. Ready-rolled butter puff pastry is available from delis and supermarkets — it doesn't get much simpler than that! Blue mackerel have a pretty silvery-blue skin and rich oily flesh; they aren't as popular as they deserve to be, so they're generally a bargain. Mediterranean flavours complement oilier fish beautifully. Basil oil keeps for a few days in the fridge, and is great in salad dressings or tossed through pasta or steamed vegetables.

To make the basil oil, blanch the basil in plenty of rapidly boiling salted water for 30 seconds, then refresh immediately in iced water. Drain, squeeze out excess water and chop roughly. Place in a mortar with the garlic, lemon juice, salt and pepper and pound with a pestle to form a paste. Stir in the oil and set aside.

Preheat the oven to 200°C (fan-forced). Roll the pastry out to a 2–3 mm thickness and cut six 12 cm × 6 cm rectangles. Place the pastry rectangles on a baking tray lined with baking paper. Spread the tomato slices evenly over the pastry and arrange the anchovies and olives on top. Sprinkle with lemon zest and drizzle with a little oil. Bake for 8–12 minutes, until the pastry is golden and crisp.

Meanwhile, trim the thin top and bottom off each mackerel fillet, then cut in half by slicing either side of the central bloodline, discarding the bloodline and pin-bones. Check the skin for any remaining scales.

Remove the tarts from the oven and place a piece of fish on each one, skin-side up. Return to the oven for about 2 minutes, until the fish is just cooked through.

Place the tarts on warm plates, drizzle with basil oil and serve.

Recipe by
Tony Bilson

WHOLE BAKED SNAPPER

SERVES 6

pinch of saffron threads

3 tablespoons Pernod

1 × 1.5–2 kg snapper, gilled,
gutted and scaled

salt flakes and freshly ground
white pepper, to taste

4 tablespoons basil leaves, thinly sliced

olive oil, for oiling dish

green salad, for serving

crusty bread, for serving

Herbed oil

200 ml extra virgin olive oil

3 cloves garlic, crushed

3 golden shallots, finely chopped

1 tablespoon strained lemon juice

1 tablespoon Dijon mustard

2 tablespoons marjoram leaves,
finely chopped

1 tablespoon thyme leaves, finely chopped

ALTERNATIVE SPECIES:
coral trout; red emperor; salmon; trout

People are often daunted by cooking whole fish, but this recipe from Tony Bilson is super easy. What's more, it looks very impressive sitting on a platter in the centre of the table, and can also be served cold or at room temperature. Tony describes this as a classic lunch dish, best served with a green salad and lots of crusty bread to soak up all the delicious cooking juices. Ideally, start a day ahead to allow time for soaking the saffron in the Pernod overnight.

Soak the saffron threads in the Pernod, preferably overnight.

To make the herbed oil, combine all the ingredients and set aside.

Preheat the oven to 180°C (fan-forced).

Wipe the fish with a clean, damp cloth inside and out, being sure to remove any blood from the belly cavity. Check for remaining scales and rinse the belly cavity with a little cold water to remove any traces of blood. Pat dry. Using a sharp knife, score both sides with two diagonal cuts just through to the bone. Using kitchen scissors, trim off the side, top and bottom fins. Sprinkle generously with salt and pepper on both sides and in the belly cavity, then place the basil in the cavity. Place the fish in a large, oiled baking dish. Place a spoonful of herbed oil in the belly cavity and spoon the rest evenly over the top of the fish. Pour the Pernod and saffron over the top.

Cook the fish for 20–30 minutes, depending on size, basting occasionally. To see if it's cooked, gently lift the flesh around the top fin: it should be moist and come away easily from the bone. Remove the fish from the oven, cover loosely with foil and set aside for 10 minutes.

Place the fish on a large platter and spoon the cooking juices over the top. Serve with a green salad and crusty bread.

COULIBIAC

Coulibiac, a traditional Russian fish pie, was popularised in French cooking by Auguste Escoffier. Today it's usually made with salmon, rice, mushrooms and hard-boiled eggs, though originally it often included sturgeon meat or marrow from a sturgeon's spinal cord. It isn't a difficult dish, though there are a number of steps and it's essential that you read through the entire recipe before starting it.

Damien Pignolet is one of the masters of classical French cooking in Australia; his research is thorough and he writes very precise recipes, so there's no one better to lead us step-by-step through this dish. Traditionally, the filling wasn't wrapped in crêpes, but this helps to hold everything together. Thaw the pastry just before you're ready to use it and keep it as cold as possible. This recipe is best made with a thick piece of salmon from the head end of the fish.

Preheat the oven to 120°C (fan-forced). Melt the butter over low heat and cook the onion, without colouring, for 10 minutes, stirring frequently. Add the mushrooms, salt and pepper and cook, covered, for a further 10 minutes, stirring occasionally. Remove the lid and continue cooking until most of the liquid has evaporated, then spread out the mushroom mixture on a plate to cool.

Place the rice in a jug, cover with cold water, then pour it off. Repeat twice more. Drain well and place in an ovenproof saucepan with 1 cup (250 ml) of cold water. Bring slowly to the boil and watch until little craters appear in the rice, then cover with the lid and place in the oven for 11 minutes. Remove from the oven and place a double thickness of paper towel on the surface of the rice. Replace the lid and leave for 15 minutes, then remove the paper towel and, using a fork, lightly fluff up the rice. Set aside to cool, then mix the dill through the rice.

Cut the fish in half horizontally to make two thinner pieces. Lay a 30 cm × 50 cm sheet of baking paper on a work surface with one of the shorter sides closest to you. Lay 2 crêpes in the centre of the paper, overlapping them by 8 cm. Remove a quarter of the rice and set it aside. Divide the remaining rice into two portions.

On the crêpe closest to you, starting at the centre of the overlap, spread one portion of the rice into a rectangle the same size as the piece of salmon. Sprinkle both sides of the salmon with salt and pepper and place a piece on top of the rice. Cover with the mushroom mixture and press down gently. Arrange egg slices down the centre of the mushrooms, then top with the reserved quarter of the rice and another piece of salmon. Press gently then cover with the remaining portion of rice, pressing the rice gently onto the salmon to cover it completely. Brush the exposed crêpe with beaten egg. Fold the crêpe closest to you to partially cover the filling. Fold the remaining crêpe over the top to tightly enclose the filling, adding an additional strip of crêpe if need be to completely cover the filling. Fold the baking paper around the parcel and refrigerate for 20 minutes.

Preheat the oven to 220°C (fan-forced). Dust a rolling pin lightly with flour and, on a sheet of lightly floured baking paper, roll out the pastry to 50 cm long. Place the wrapped parcel on the pastry and measure how much will be needed to enclose it with an overlap to seal (if need be, roll the pastry slightly thinner); trim off the excess pastry in one strip and set it aside.

Remove the paper from the parcel and place the parcel upside-down in the centre of the pastry. Brush the exposed pastry with beaten egg. Fold the pastry up and over the parcel, folding in the ends to completely enclose and brushing with beaten egg where necessary to help seal. Press the pastry well to seal wherever it overlaps. Turn the parcel over so that the join is underneath.

Cut the reserved trimmed pastry into three long strips and plait to make a braid, stretching the pastry slightly if necessary so that it's as long as the coulibiac. Brush beaten egg along the centre of the coulibiac and lay the braid along the egg wash, tucking the ends of the braid underneath to secure.

Wrap baking paper around the coulibiac and refrigerate for 10 minutes. Meanwhile, place a large baking tray in the oven to preheat.

Remove coulibiac from the fridge and place on the baking tray. Unwrap, leaving the baking paper underneath. Brush all over with beaten egg. Bake for 10 minutes, then reduce the temperature to 180°C (fan-forced) and bake for at least a further 20 minutes, until golden. Remove from the oven and leave to rest in a warm place for 5–10 minutes.

Slide the coulibiac off the paper onto a platter and, using a serrated knife, trim off the ends and cut into six portions. Using a cake server or wide spatula, transfer the slices to plates and serve.

Recipe by
Damien Pignolet

SERVES 6

50 g unsalted butter

1 small brown onion, finely diced

225 g button mushrooms, caps only, finely diced

salt flakes and freshly ground white pepper, to taste

½ cup (100 g) jasmine rice

1 handful roughly chopped dill

1 × 500 g piece salmon fillet, skin off, pin-boned and belly flap trimmed off

2 × 24 cm diameter crêpes (see Basics)

1 egg, hard-boiled and cut into slices about 5 mm thick

1 egg, lightly beaten with a pinch of salt

plain flour, for dusting

1 × 27 cm square sheet butter puff pastry (see Chefs' ingredients)

ALTERNATIVE SPECIES:
ocean trout

Recipe by
Eugenio Riva

GOLDBAND SNAPPER FILLETS BAKED 'AL CARTOCCIO'

SERVES 6

1 large eggplant (aubergine)

large pinch of saffron threads

1 cup (250 ml) extra virgin olive oil

1 red onion, finely diced

1 large yellow capsicum (pepper), finely diced

1 large red capsicum (pepper), finely diced

3 cloves garlic, minced

salt flakes and freshly ground black pepper, to taste

3 zucchini (courgettes), finely diced

6 × 180 g pieces goldband snapper fillets, skin on and pin-boned

12 sprigs thyme

3 tablespoons strained lemon juice

crusty bread, for serving

ALTERNATIVE SPECIES:
bass groper; red mullet; snapper

Fish is often wrapped in baking paper, foil, leaves or even bark, to help protect its delicate flesh and keep it moist while it steams in its own juices. When the diners open the parcels at the table, all the delicious aromas are released. Eugenio Riva often served fish cooked this way at the popular Ristorante Riva. If you let the vegetables cool completely first, you can wrap the parcels a few hours ahead of time and leave them in the fridge, ready to go – just remove them from the fridge about 20 minutes before cooking, so they come to room temperature.

Preheat the oven to 200°C (fan-forced).

Halve the eggplant and scoop out most of the flesh, leaving about 1 cm of flesh on the skin. Chop the eggplant skin into small dice, discarding the scooped-out flesh.

Soak the saffron in 1 teaspoon of hot water for 5 minutes, then combine with the oil. Heat a large frying pan over high heat and add the saffron oil. When hot, add the onion and stir for 1 minute. Add both the capsicums and garlic and stir for a further minute, then add the eggplant and a generous amount of salt and stir for 3 minutes. Reduce the heat to medium, add the zucchini and stir for a further 3 minutes. Remove the pan from the heat and set it aside.

Cut six sheets of foil, each large enough to wrap one piece of fish completely. Cut six sheets of baking paper, each slightly longer than the sheets of foil. Lay the foil pieces on a work surface, shiny-side up, then top each one with a sheet of baking paper.

Check the fish skin for any remaining scales, then sprinkle generously with salt and pepper on each side. Place a piece of fish on each sheet of baking paper, skin-side down. Top with the vegetable mixture, add 2 sprigs of thyme and drizzle with lemon juice. Fold the two long sides of the paper and foil over in a couple of folds above the fish, without pushing it against the fish, then fold the ends over to form a secure package so that the steam and juices can't escape.

Place the parcels on a baking tray and cook for 15–20 minutes, depending on the thickness of the fillets, until the flesh flakes easily when tested with a fork.

Place the parcels on plates for diners to open at the table. Serve with crusty bread to soak up the juices.

BARBECUING

Barbecuing is the oldest form of cooking. Traditionally, food was cooked over an open fire, hot coals or embers; today, a flat or ridged char-grill heated by electricity or gas is more common. Most barbecue recipes can also be cooked in a frying pan if you don't have a barbecue or char-grill pan.

Cooking times will vary, depending on the thickness and the density of the seafood's flesh. Fish is cooked when it turns opaque. Sashimi-grade seafood can be seared on the barbecue and served still rare in the centre.

TIPS FOR SUCCESSFUL BARBECUING

* **Remove seafood from the fridge 15–30 minutes before cooking** and allow it to come to room temperature. This is particularly important if fish is whole, quite thick or being served rare.

* **Don't place seafood over a flaming fire.** If you are using a wood-fuelled barbecue, allow the fire to burn down to a bed of glowing embers before cooking. Even if you are using a flat metal plate, flames coming into contact with the plate can create hot spots, and you'll get a far more even heat distribution without flames. The centre of the plate is usually the hottest part; if the fish is colouring too quickly (before it has a chance to cook inside), move it to the edge of the plate.

* **If cooking with gas, a medium flame is best. If cooking with electricity, a high setting is best.** The heat from an electric barbecue tends to be less intense than that from gas or wood.

* **Wipe off excess marinade before cooking.** Otherwise, the fish may stew rather than grill.

* **Score whole fish through the thickest part of the flesh to the bone.** Make a few cuts on both sides to allow even heat penetration.

* **Oil seafood well before placing it on the barbecue.** This will help prevent sticking; oiling the food rather than the barbecue helps to minimise excess smoke.

* **Turn the fish as little as possible to avoid damaging its delicate flesh.** Cook one side, then turn and cook the other side. With kebabs or thick steaks, place each of the four sides in contact with the grill once only, cooking each side before moving on to the next.

* **If cooking fillets with their skin on, cook them skin-side down first.** Cook on the skin-side until fish is opaque almost all the way through, as the skin helps protect the delicate flesh from the heat, then turn over to just colour the other side.

* **Wrap the fish to protect it from drying out.** Foil, leaves (such as vine or banana leaves) or damp paperbark can be used to wrap fish. The unwrapped leaves or bark also make an attractive base on which to serve the cooked fish.

Recipe by
Shaun Presland

TUNA TATAKI WITH
SESAME SOY DRESSING

SERVES 6 AS AN ENTRÉE

¼ daikon (white radish),
cut into very fine matchsticks

1 × 500 g piece sashimi-grade yellowfin tuna

fine sea salt and freshly ground
white pepper, to taste

vegetable oil, for oiling

100 g mesclun

¼ head baby frisée

3 red cherry tomatoes, quartered

3 yellow cherry tomatoes, quartered

¼ telegraph (long) cucumber,
seeded and cut into batons

Sesame soy dressing

1½ teaspoons Japanese mustard powder

4 tablespoons soy sauce

4 tablespoons Japanese rice vinegar

½ teaspoon caster sugar

salt flakes, to taste

1 tablespoon grapeseed oil

1 tablespoon sesame oil

½ small white onion, finely chopped

ALTERNATIVE SPECIES:
bigeye tuna

Tataki is a classic Japanese way of preparing fish or meat, in which you sear it briefly in a very hot pan, and serve it thinly sliced. The cooked outside contrasts beautifully with the raw interior. The traditional accompaniments, a vinegar-based dressing and pounded ginger, give the dish its name (*tataki* is Japanese for 'pound'). Here Shaun Presland, the first Australian Caucasian chef to be honoured with the title of Sushi Chef, adds his spin with a sesame soy dressing. Japanese mustard powder is sold in Asian grocery stores, but you could always use Keen's mustard powder instead. Leftover dressing will keep for a week in the fridge and is great on any salad. If possible, drain the chopped onion in a sieve in the fridge overnight; this will remove some of its bitterness. A long, thin piece of tuna, about 20 cm long, 8 cm thick and 4 cm wide, is ideal for this recipe.

Soak the daikon in iced water until crisp.

Remove any remaining skin and bloodline from the tuna. Sprinkle the tuna very generously with salt and pepper and set it aside at room temperature for 20 minutes.

Preheat a barbecue or char-grill pan on the highest setting. Half-fill a bowl that's large enough to hold the tuna with water and ice. Rub the tuna with oil, then sear it for about 30 seconds each side, until cooked 1 mm in on all sides. Remove the tuna from the heat and submerge it in the iced water for a few seconds to stop it cooking any further, then carefully lift it out of the water and pat it dry. Place the tuna on a plate lined with paper towel, then cover with plastic wrap and refrigerate for a good 20 minutes.

Meanwhile, to make the sesame soy dressing, dissolve the mustard powder in 2 teaspoons of warm water. Combine the soy sauce, rice vinegar, caster sugar and salt and stir until the sugar dissolves, then mix in the mustard paste. Whisk in the grapeseed and sesame oils and stir in the onion. Set aside.

Using a very sharp knife, thinly slice the tuna across the grain on the diagonal. Fan the tuna slices around each plate.

Drain the daikon and pat dry. Toss the mesclun, frisée, tomatoes and cucumber with enough sesame soy dressing to coat and place in the centre of each plate. Drizzle a little more dressing over the tuna and top with the daikon.

Recipe by
David Thompson

GRILLED BARRAMUNDI CURRY

SERVES 2

2 × 180 g pieces barramundi fillet,
skin on and pin-boned

4 × 20 cm lengths banana leaf, wiped with
a clean, damp cloth on both sides

½ cup (125 ml) coconut cream (see Basics)

1 large handful Thai basil leaves

10 kaffir lime leaves, finely shredded

steamed jasmine rice, for serving

Red curry paste

2 teaspoons Thai shrimp paste (gapi)

16 dried long red chillies, seeded and
soaked in cold water with a pinch of salt
for 10 minutes, then drained

large pinch of salt flakes

4 tablespoons finely chopped lemongrass,
white part only

2 tablespoons chopped galangal

4 tablespoons chopped red shallots

6 tablespoons chopped garlic

2 teaspoons finely chopped kaffir lime zest

2 teaspoons scraped and chopped
coriander root

Grated coconut mixture

⅔ cup (160 ml) coconut cream (see Basics)

½ cup (150 g) Red curry paste (see above)

3 tablespoons grated palm sugar,
more or less, to taste

3 tablespoons fish sauce (see Chefs'
ingredients), more or less to taste

1 cup (80 g) freshly grated coconut

ALTERNATIVE SPECIES:
snapper; yellowtail kingfish; prawn; rocklobster

David Thompson is the master of Thai food, a diligent researcher and enthusiastic teacher who loves sharing his passion for Thai food and culture. Despite being busy with his nahm restaurants in London and Bangkok, he conducts occasional classes at the Seafood School, which are always exhilarating. Of course, it's important to taste all dishes as you cook, but in Thai cuisine even more so as the seasoning very much depends on personal taste; with ingredients such as fish sauce and palm sugar, add just a little, then taste and add a little more if you think it's needed. Like all Thai dishes, this would traditionally be served alongside several other dishes as part of a shared meal. Store leftover curry paste in the fridge for up to 2 weeks, tightly sealed in an airtight container with plastic wrap pressed against the surface.

To make the red curry paste, wrap the shrimp paste in foil and place it under a hot overhead grill for a couple of minutes. Place the chillies in a mortar with the salt and pound with a pestle to form a paste. Continue pounding, adding the remaining ingredients one by one in the order given and finishing with the shrimp paste, to form a smooth paste.

To make the grated coconut mixture, place the coconut cream in a small frying pan and bring to the boil. Boil it for a moment, then add ½ cup (150 g) of the red curry paste, reduce the heat slightly and simmer, stirring constantly, for about 5 minutes, until it's fragrant and the coconut cream begins to split. Stir in the palm sugar, fish sauce and grated coconut and continue cooking for at least another 5 minutes, until the coconut is tender and the paste is quite dry and tastes smooth and cooked (if the mixture becomes too dry before it's cooked, add a little extra water or coconut cream). Set the coconut mixture aside.

Check the fish for any remaining scales. Lay two pieces of banana leaf on a work surface, dull-side down, then top each with a second piece of banana leaf and smear over a quarter of the coconut cream. Sprinkle over a quarter of the basil leaves, a quarter of the kaffir lime leaves and half of the grated coconut mixture. Repeat the layering of coconut cream, basil and kaffir lime leaves. Place a fish fillet on each leaf and repeat the layering but in reverse (kaffir lime leaves, basil, coconut cream, grated coconut mixture, kaffir lime leaves, basil, coconut cream). Fold the top banana leaf around each fish fillet, then wrap each parcel quite tightly using the bottom banana leaf; the outer leaf should char during the cooking, while the inner leaf is used to serve.

Preheat a barbecue or char-grill pan. Cook the parcels for 10–20 minutes, until the outer leaf is well charred. Remove the outer banana leaf. Open up the inner leaf and serve with steamed rice on the side.

Recipe by
Haru Inukai

GRILLED STICKY-RICE-STUFFED GARFISH WRAPPED IN BAMBOO LEAVES WITH CHILLI VINAIGRETTE

SERVES 6 AS AN ENTRÉE

12 garfish fillets, skin on and pin-boned

2 tablespoons Japanese plum paste

1 tablespoon yukari seasoning

12 fresh bamboo leaves, wiped with a clean, damp cloth on both sides

grapeseed oil, for brushing

Sticky rice

1 cup (200 g) white glutinous rice

1 kaffir lime leaf

pinch of salt

25 ml sake

Chilli vinaigrette

juice of ½ lime, strained

juice of ½ lemon, strained

2.5 cm piece ginger, grated

1 small clove garlic, crushed

45 ml Japanese rice vinegar

3 tablespoons grapeseed oil

1 small red chilli, seeded and finely chopped

2 teaspoons finely chopped coriander

1½ teaspoons honey

1 kaffir lime leaf, very finely chopped

salt flakes and freshly ground white pepper, to taste

2½ tablespoons fish sauce (see Chefs' ingredients)

15 ml soy sauce

15 ml mirin

½ teaspoon caster sugar

ALTERNATIVE SPECIES:
small whiting

When Haru Inukai was chef at Restaurant VII he taught several classes at the Seafood School, and these delicious parcels were among his recipes. Glutinous rice, also called sticky rice, is a short-grained Asian rice that is especially sticky when cooked. It's important to leave it covered while cooking and resting, or the texture won't be right. The rice is available from Asian grocery stores, as are Japanese plum paste and yukari seasoning (which may be labelled 'mishima yukari seasoning for rice'). Bamboo leaves can be a little harder to come by, though they are available from some Asian grocery stores. Alternatively, if you don't have any bamboo in your neighbourhood, ask your local nursery if you can pick a few leaves; you want them to be around the same width as the garfish fillets. You'll need kitchen string to tie up the parcels.

To make the chilli vinaigrette, place all the ingredients in a bowl and whisk to combine. This makes 1 cup (250 ml; leftovers will keep refrigerated for up to 1 week.)

To cook the sticky rice, place all the ingredients and 1¼ cups (310 ml) of cold water in a saucepan over low heat and gradually increase the heat to bring to the boil. Cover, reduce the heat and simmer the rice for 20 minutes. Remove the pan from the heat and set aside, covered, for 10 minutes.

Check the fish for any remaining scales. Lay the fillets, skin-side down, on a work surface. Spread the plum paste over the flesh side of the fillets and sprinkle the yukari seasoning on top. Place a 1 cm-wide strip of sticky rice all the way along half of the fillets and top with a second fillet, skin-side up, to create six 'sandwiches'. Lay 6 bamboo leaves on the work surface, shiny-side down. Brush one side of the garfish 'sandwiches' with grapeseed oil and place each one lengthways on top of a bamboo leaf, oiled-side down. Brush the top fillet with grapeseed oil and top with the remaining bamboo leaves, shiny-side up. Tie up each parcel at three evenly spaced intervals with lengths of kitchen string.

Preheat a barbecue or char-grill pan over medium heat. Cook the parcels for 3–5 minutes on each side, depending on size, until the leaves are well charred. Place a parcel on each plate, then snip and remove the string and discard the top bamboo leaves. Pour a teaspoon or so of chilli vinaigrette over each fish and serve.

TUNA BROCHETTE
À LA BISCAYENNE

Recipe by
Matthew Kemp

Brochette is the French term for anything cooked on a skewer, and Biscay is a province of the Basque Country in northern Spain, so this dish is tuna kebabs with a Spanish sauce . . . but somehow it sounds better in French, doesn't it? Matthew Kemp has a way of dressing up something simple to make it delicious, and this dish is a good example. The capsicum sauce can be made a few days ahead and warmed over low heat before serving; just add the basil leaves at the last minute. If you prefer, you can cook the capsicums on a barbecue or char-grill pan; just remember that the skin needs to be really black so you can peel it easily. You'll need long bamboo or metal skewers for this recipe – if using bamboo ones, soak them in water for 30 minutes beforehand, so they don't catch fire on the grill.

Remove any remaining skin and bloodline from the tuna. Set the tuna aside at room temperature for 15–30 minutes.

Roast the capsicums over a flame until the skins turn black on all sides. Put the capsicums in a bowl, cover tightly with plastic wrap and set aside. When the capsicums are cool enough to handle, peel them and rinse off any remaining bits of black skin without getting the capsicums too wet. Split the capsicums down one side and open them out flat. Scrape away the seeds and membrane, trying to keep the flesh in one piece. Pat the capsicums dry with paper towel, then slice them as finely as possible.

Heat a frying pan over low heat and add the extra virgin olive oil. When hot, add the onion, prosciutto, chilli, garlic and salt and cook until the onion is really soft but not coloured. Add the tomato paste and sugar and cook for a further 5 minutes. Add the capsicum and stir gently until it is coated with the onion mixture. Add the basil stalks and season with salt and pepper, then cover and cook for 10–15 minutes, stirring regularly. Remove the pan from the heat, then discard the basil stalks and stir in the basil leaves.

Meanwhile, preheat a barbecue or char-grill pan over medium heat. Cut the tuna into 3 cm cubes and thread them onto six skewers. Brush lightly with oil, sprinkle generously with salt, and cook until lightly coloured on all sides; the tuna should be rare in the middle.

Serve the tuna skewers on top of the capsicum mixture.

SERVES 6

1 × 1 kg piece sashimi-grade yellowfin tuna

4 red capsicums (peppers)

4 yellow capsicums (peppers)

200 ml extra virgin olive oil

1 white onion, sliced

1 × 100 g piece prosciutto, diced

1 long red chilli, seeded and sliced

2 cloves garlic, sliced

salt flakes and freshly ground
white pepper, to taste

1 teaspoon tomato paste

1 teaspoon white sugar

1 bunch basil, leaves picked and
stalks reserved

olive oil, for brushing

ALTERNATIVE SPECIES:
bonito; swordfish

GRILLED BASS GROPER WITH BROAD BEANS, ARTICHOKE HEARTS, LEEKS & ROMESCO SAUCE

Peter Doyle's cooking draws inspiration from all over Europe, and his dishes are some of the prettiest presented at the Seafood School. Often the difference between what chefs prepare and what we cook at home is simply the addition of some delicious sauces to add flavour, colour and texture. This recipe is inspired by the flavours of Spain and features romesco, a classic Spanish sauce from the coastal region of Catalonia, which is often paired with seafood. The recipe makes more sauce than you'll need for this dish, but it keeps refrigerated for up to 4 days and is delicious with any seafood, meat or vegetables. Bass groper fillets are quite thick; slicing them on the diagonal produces thinner pieces with a good cross-section of flesh and a thin strip of skin, which cook quickly and so stay moist. Leftover pieces from either end can be used for fish cakes or another dish.

To make the lemon vinaigrette, place the lemon juice in a bowl with the salt and pepper, and gradually whisk in the oil. Leftover vinaigrette will keep covered in the fridge for a week and is delicious on salad or cooked vegetables.

For the romesco sauce, preheat the oven to 200°C (fan-forced). Spread the almonds on a baking tray and set aside. Place the tomatoes and garlic on a separate oiled baking tray. Cut the tops off the capsicums and scoop out all the seeds, leaving the capsicums whole. Heat the 3 tablespoons of olive oil in a baking dish in the oven for about 10 minutes, add the capsicums and turn to coat. Place the almonds, tomatoes and garlic, and capsicums in the oven.

Cook the almonds until they're golden, about 6 minutes, watching them closely as they'll burn easily. Cook the capsicums for 10 minutes on one side, then turn them over and cook for a further 5–8 minutes on each remaining side, until blistered all over. Place the capsicums in a bowl and cover with plastic wrap. Cook the tomatoes and garlic for 20 minutes or so, until the tomatoes are soft.

Squeeze the roasted garlic cloves out of their skins into a food processor. When the capsicums and tomatoes are cool enough to handle, peel and coarsely chop them, reserving their juices.

Add the almonds, along with the capsicum and tomato and their juices plus the chilli to the food processor and pulse to blend, gradually adding the vinegar. With the motor running, gradually add the extra virgin olive oil in a steady stream. Add salt and pepper, then set the romesco sauce aside.

Blanch the broad beans in boiling salted water for 30–60 seconds, depending on their size. Remove them using a strainer, then refresh in iced water. When the beans are cool, drain and peel them. If any of the peeled beans are large, return them to boiling water and cook for a further minute, then refresh. Set the beans aside. Add the leeks to the boiling water and blanch for 3 minutes. Remove and refresh in iced water, then drain and pat them dry.

Preheat a barbecue or char-grill pan over high heat. Check the fish for any remaining scales then trim off and discard the thin belly flap. Slice the fish into six pieces on the diagonal, discarding the off-cuts from either end. Sprinkle the fish with pepper and brush with oil on both sides, then brush the barbecue or char-grill with oil. Cook the fish, skin-side down, for about 2 minutes, until lightly golden, then turn over and cook for another minute or so, until it feels firm to the touch but is still moist in the centre. Transfer the fish to a warmed plate and set aside in a warm place to rest.

Meanwhile, place the broad beans, leeks and artichokes in a steamer set over a saucepan of simmering water to gently warm through.

To serve, arrange the vegetables on plates, sprinkle liberally with salt and pepper and drizzle with lemon vinaigrette. Spoon some romesco sauce onto each plate. Lean a piece of fish on the vegetables, top with chilli, drizzle with extra lemon vinaigrette and sprinkle with salt. Serve with a little more of the romesco sauce.

Recipe by
Peter Doyle

SERVES 6

250 g baby broad beans, podded

12 baby leeks, washed well

1 × 1.2 kg piece bass groper fillet, skin on and pin-boned

salt flakes and freshly ground black pepper, to taste

olive oil, for brushing

9 preserved artichoke hearts in olive oil, drained and halved

1 red serrano chilli, or similar hot chilli, seeded and chopped

Lemon vinaigrette

2½ tablespoons strained lemon juice

salt flakes and freshly ground black pepper, to taste

1 cup (250 ml) extra virgin olive oil

Romesco sauce

2 tablespoons blanched almonds, roughly chopped

2 roma (plum) tomatoes, halved

3 cloves garlic, skin on

2 red capsicums (peppers)

3 tablespoons olive oil, plus extra for oiling

4 long dried red chillies, coarsely chopped

3 tablespoons white wine vinegar (see Chefs' ingredients)

300 ml extra virgin olive oil

salt flakes and freshly ground black pepper, to taste

ALTERNATIVE SPECIES:
mulloway; swordfish

DEEP-FRYING

When it's done properly, deep-frying is a great way to cook seafood: it's fast, cooking most seafood in less than 5 minutes; it quickly seals the surface, locking in flavour and moisture; and it adds appealing crunch, colour and aroma. You can deep-fry in olive oil, peanut oil, vegetable oil or ghee, depending on the flavour you want to achieve.

If you want to re-use the cooking oil, filter the cooled oil through a coffee filter or muslin-lined sieve to remove any food particles and sediment. Store in a cool dark place and discard after a week or four uses (whichever comes first). Dispose of the oil in an environmentally safe manner – never down the sink.

There are a few essential safety tips to heed when deep-frying. Don't drop food into hot oil; carefully slide it into the oil from the side of the pan to prevent splashing. Avoid reaching over or across containers of hot oil, and never carry or move containers of hot oil or oil that is on fire. Extinguish oil fires by sliding a lid over the top of the container and leaving it there until the flames have been extinguished and the oil is cool. It's also a good idea to keep a small fire blanket in the kitchen, just in case.

TIPS FOR SUCCESSFUL DEEP-FRYING

* **Don't over-fill fryers.** Don't fill electric fryers beyond their maximum level; if using a wok or saucepan, only half-fill them.

* **Oil is usually heated to around 180–190°C for deep-frying**. To test, drop in a cube of bread: it should brown in 15 seconds. If the oil smokes, it's too hot and food is likely to cook on the outside while the inside stays raw. If the oil is too cold, the food will absorb it and become greasy and soggy.

* **Don't overload the fryer.** If you do, the oil temperature will drop and take too long to recover, meaning the food will absorb oil and become soggy. Cook in batches if necessary, and always allow time for the oil to return to temperature before adding the next batch.

* **Dry uncoated seafood on paper towel before deep-frying.** This will prevent the oil from spitting.

* **Don't overcook seafood.** It's ready as soon as the flesh turns opaque and the coating is golden brown.

* **Drain deep-fried seafood well**. Lay it on paper towel to remove excess oil.

61

Recipe by
Alex Herbert

FISH & CHIPS

SERVES 4

220 g self-raising flour

80 g plain flour, plus extra for dusting

2 tablespoons olive oil

2 tablespoons white wine vinegar
(see Chefs' ingredients)

360 ml beer

4 egg whites

salt flakes, to taste

vegetable oil, for deep-frying

8 × 125 g flathead fillets,
skin off and pin-boned

Tartare sauce (see Basics), for serving

lemon cheeks, for serving

oven fries, for serving

ALTERNATIVE SPECIES:
whiting

What would a seafood cookbook be without a great fish and chips recipe? At her restaurant bird cow fish, Alex Herbert served a particularly delicious version of this classic. Flathead is the best Australian fish for fish and chips, as it's so moist and flaky. It's good to know that even chefs 'cheat' by using frozen French fries – they do give the best, most consistent result (Alex uses Edgell straight-cut shoestring fries). So all you have to worry about is whisking up the batter and making a simple tartare sauce, which is quick and so much better than anything you can buy. Cook the fries in the oven while you're cooking the fish, or if you prefer to deep-fry them, cook them first, then just reheat them by dipping them back into the hot oil for a minute once the fish is cooked. You'll have to cook the fish in batches to avoid overcrowding, and it is best served as soon as it's cooked, so put the first lot on the table and tell people to dig in while you cook the other batches; each batch only takes a few minutes. The fish can also be kept warm on the bottom shelf of the oven for a few minutes.

Sift the flours together into a bowl and make a well in the centre. Combine the olive oil and vinegar and whisk it into the flour, then whisk in the beer, mixing until just combined; the batter should still be a little lumpy. Cover the bowl with plastic wrap and set aside to rest for 1 hour at room temperature.

Whisk the egg whites and salt until stiff peaks form. Fold the egg whites through the batter.

Preheat the vegetable oil to 180°C (see page 61). Dust the fish lightly with the extra flour, shaking off any excess. Dip the fish into the batter, then lower it carefully into the oil and deep-fry for a minute or two, until the underside is well coloured, then turn and fry the other side for another minute or two, until the batter is well coloured all over. Test the fish by inserting a metal skewer into the thickest part: if the skewer is hot to touch, then the fish is cooked.

Sprinkle the fish with salt and serve immediately with tartare sauce, lemon cheeks and fries sprinkled with salt.

Recipe by
Mark Jensen

SALAD OF FRIED SEA MULLET, GREEN MANGO & MANGOSTEENS

SERVES 4

1 teaspoon sesame seeds

vegetable oil, for deep-frying

500 g sea mullet fillets, skin on, pin-boned and cut into bite-sized pieces

2 tablespoons potato starch

2 green mangos, finely shaved

3 mangosteens, segmented

¼ small red onion, very thinly sliced

3 tablespoons dried shrimp, soaked in boiling water for 10 minutes, then drained and squeezed

1 small handful mint leaves, roughly chopped

1 small handful perilla leaves, roughly chopped

1 small handful Vietnamese mint leaves, roughly chopped

1 small red chilli, thinly sliced

steamed jasmine rice, for serving

Vietnamese dressing

3 tablespoons Vietnamese fish sauce

1 tablespoon soy sauce

3 tablespoons shao hsing (see page 108)

2 teaspoons caster sugar

2 teaspoons sambal oelek (chilli paste)

4 cm piece lemongrass, white part only, very finely chopped

juice of 1 lime, strained

ALTERNATIVE SPECIES:
Australian sardine; bonito

Mark Jensen learnt to cook Vietnamese food from his parents-in-law, who owned Vietnamese restaurants in Cabramatta. His dishes are authentic, but with a modern approach that makes them more accessible to home cooks. Vietnamese food is defined by an abundance of fresh herbs: here it's Vietnamese mint, perilla (also called shiso) and mint. The Vietnamese mint and perilla are available from Asian grocery stores, but if these are unavailable, you can substitute other Asian herbs such as coriander or Thai basil. Mangosteens are a seasonal fruit with a thick, dark red skin and sweet, tangy white flesh; if unavailable, use lychees. Vietnamese fish sauce is lighter in colour and flavour than the more common Thai fish sauce, but you can use a Thai one if that's what you have. If you aren't a fan of chilli heat, you can always leave out the chilli garnish.

To make the Vietnamese dressing, place the fish sauce, soy sauce, shao hsing, sugar and ½ cup (125 ml) of water in a saucepan and mix well. Bring to the boil, then remove from the heat and set aside to cool. Stir in the sambal oelek, lemongrass and lime juice.

Place the sesame seeds on a baking tray under an overhead grill and heat them, stirring frequently, until they are slightly coloured and aromatic; watch them closely as they can burn quickly.

Preheat the oil to 180°C (see page 61). Check the fish for any remaining scales, then lightly dust with potato starch, shaking off any excess. Working in batches, carefully lower the fish into the oil and deep-fry for a minute or two until the underside is crisp, then turn and fry the other side for another minute or so, until the centre is just cooked. Drain on paper towel.

Combine the mango, mangosteen, onion, shrimp, mint, perilla, Vietnamese mint and toasted sesame seeds in a bowl with ½ cup (125 ml) of the dressing. Add the fish and toss gently to combine.

Arrange the salad on a plate, sprinkle the chilli over the top and serve with steamed jasmine rice alongside.

FRIED LEMON & ALMOND COATED KING GEORGE WHITING WITH WARM CRAB SALAD

Recipe by
Justin North

Crumbed whiting is a classic Aussie dish. Justin North makes it special by using King George whiting, one of Australia's most-prized fish. The largest and most expensive of the whitings, it's caught mainly off South Australia. It isn't always available, but you could substitute any of the whiting family. Crabmeat is available frozen from good fishmongers. Salad onions are long, thin green onions with a small developed bulb.

To make the caponata dressing, preheat the oven to 180°C (fan-forced). Halve the capsicum, discarding the seeds and membrane, and place it on a baking tray, cut-side up. Top with the garlic and thyme and drizzle with the olive oil and vinegar. Cover with foil and cook for about 15 minutes, until the skin blisters. Place the capsicum in a bowl, cover with plastic wrap and set aside. Strain the cooking juices into a separate bowl. When the capsicum is cool enough to handle, peel and cut it into small dice. Place the capsicum in the bowl with the strained cooking juices. Add the chives, anchovies, capers and lemon zest and mix well. Set the caponata dressing aside.

Place three bowls on the benchtop: whisk the eggs and milk together in one; combine the breadcrumbs, ground almonds, lemon zest, salt and pepper in the next; and place the flour in the last, seasoning it with salt and pepper. Check the fish for any remaining scales and trim off the ends and belly flap, then lightly dust the fish with the seasoned flour, shaking off any excess. Dip it into the egg mixture, drain off any excess, then roll in the breadcrumb mixture, patting it on well. Refrigerate until needed.

For the warm crab salad, use a small sharp knife to remove the lemon rind and pith, then hold the lemon over a bowl and cut down either side of the white membranes to release the segments. Cut the lemon segments into small pieces and set aside. Blanch the asparagus in boiling salted water for 1 minute. Drain well, then place it in a frying pan over very low heat with the remaining ingredients and leave to warm through.

Preheat the vegetable oil to 190°C (see page 61). Carefully lower the fish into the oil and deep-fry for a minute or two until the underside is golden brown, then turn and fry the other side for another minute or two. Drain the fish on paper towel and sprinkle with salt, pepper and a few drops of lemon juice.

Arrange the crab salad on plates and top with the fish. Drizzle with the caponata dressing and serve immediately.

ALTERNATIVE SPECIES:
other whiting; flathead; snapper

SERVES 6

6 eggs

150 ml milk

300 g fine fresh breadcrumbs
(see Chefs' ingredients)

150 g ground almonds

finely grated zest and strained juice of 1 lemon

salt flakes and freshly ground
white pepper, to taste

150 g plain flour

6 × 100 g King George whiting fillets,
skin on and pin-boned

vegetable oil, for deep-frying

Caponata dressing

1 large red capsicum (pepper)

1 clove garlic, bruised

2 sprigs thyme

1 tablespoon extra virgin olive oil

2 teaspoons sherry vinegar

1 bunch chives, finely snipped

80 g anchovy fillets in oil (see Chefs'
ingredients), drained and finely chopped

30 g salted baby capers, rinsed and dried

finely grated zest of 1 lemon

Warm crab salad

1 lemon

24 green asparagus spears, peeled and sliced

12 vine-ripened tomatoes, peeled,
seeded and diced

600 g cooked crabmeat, checked for
cartilage and well drained (see page 179)

1 bunch salad onions, thinly sliced

150 ml extra virgin olive oil

salt flakes and freshly ground
white pepper, to taste

Recipe by
Ryuichi Yoshii

CORAL COD MIZORE-STYLE IN BONITO STOCK

SERVES 6 AS AN ENTRÉE

1 leek, white part only, cut into very thin shreds and washed well

½ carrot, cut into very thin shreds

½ Lebanese cucumber, peeled, seeded and cut into very thin shreds

6 × 80 g pieces coral cod fillet, skin on and pin-boned

1 cup (150 g) potato starch

vegetable oil, for deep-frying

300 g daikon (white radish), finely grated and squeezed to remove excess moisture

½ bunch chives, very finely snipped

Bonito stock

300 ml water

1 tablespoon instant dashi powder, more or less, to taste

2½ tablespoons soy sauce

2½ tablespoons mirin

ALTERNATIVE SPECIES:
barramundi; bar rock cod; blue-eye trevalla; snapper

Ryuichi Yoshii was one of the first Japanese chefs to introduce Australians to modern Japanese food, beyond raw fish, tempura and teppanyaki. *Mizore* is the Japanese word for sleet, which the grated daikon in this dish resembles. Deep-frying seals in the fish's moisture and flavour and then a quick dunk in boiling water washes away any excess oil. The fish is finished in a delicate stock made from dashi, a Japanese stock powder based on dried bonito flakes and kelp, which is available from Asian grocery stores. Yoshii-san likes to garnish this dish with butterflies carved from carrots; you can create your own carved vegetable garnish if you wish.

To make the bonito stock, bring the water to the boil. Stir in half the dashi powder, taste and, if you like it a little stronger, add some more; you may not need it all. Add the soy sauce and mirin. Return to the boil, then remove the pan from the heat and set aside.

Rinse the leek, carrot and cucumber shreds in cold water, then drain and soak in fresh water to crisp up. Check the fish for any remaining scales. Cut each piece into three even-sized pieces and cut five slits along each piece, about two-thirds of the way through. Brush the potato starch over the fish, ensuring it goes into the slits.

Bring a large saucepan of water to the boil. Preheat the oil to 180°C (see page 61). Carefully lower the fish into the oil and deep-fry for a minute or so, until the underside is light brown, then turn and fry the other side for another minute. Remove the fish from the oil and dip it into the boiling water for 2 seconds to remove excess oil. Set aside on paper towel.

Bring the bonito stock to the boil. Add the grated daikon and boil for a further minute. Add the fish, reduce the heat a little to a gentle boil and cook for a further 2 minutes.

Remove the fish from the stock and place in the centre of shallow bowls. Drain the leek, carrot and cucumber and pat dry. Pour some bonito stock over the top of the fish, place a mound of leek mixture on top and sprinkle with chives; add more bonito stock, to taste, then serve immediately.

Recipe by
Christine Manfield

ESCABECHE

SERVES 4 AS AN ENTRÉE

1 teaspoon cumin seeds

2 tablespoons plain flour

2 teaspoons salt flakes

½ teaspoon chilli powder

12 small red mullet fillets,
skin on and pin-boned

300 ml extra virgin olive oil

8 cloves garlic, finely chopped

½ cup (125 ml) red wine vinegar
(see Chefs' ingredients)

2 fresh bay leaves

2 sprigs thyme

1 small red chilli, thinly sliced

1 teaspoon Spanish unsmoked sweet
paprika (see Chefs' ingredients)

½ teaspoon freshly ground
black pepper

coriander, dill, mint, flat-leaf parsley
and oregano leaves, roughly chopped,
for serving

crusty bread, for serving

ALTERNATIVE SPECIES:
Australian sardine; mullet; school whiting

Escabeche is a Spanish dish of fried fish covered in a hot vinegar marinade and typically served cold; variations of the dish are popular in Italy, Portugal, France, North Africa, South America and the Philippines. Originally, this technique was used to preserve the fish, which would have had a much stronger flavour than Christine Manfield's modern version here. The fish can be eaten at room temperature as soon as the marinade has cooled down, but it can also be kept, refrigerated, for up to 3 days.

Place the cumin seeds in a small frying pan (without any oil) and cook over medium heat, stirring frequently, until fragrant. Watch them closely as they burn quickly. Grind the roasted cumin seeds to a powder using a mortar and pestle or spice grinder, then set aside.

Combine the flour, salt and chilli powder. Check the fish for any remaining scales, then dust it lightly in the flour mixture, shaking off any excess.

Heat a frying pan and add 100 ml of the oil. When hot, fry the fish in small batches for 2–3 minutes, until golden and cooked through. Place the cooked fish in a single layer in a small non-reactive dish.

Combine the garlic, vinegar, bay leaves, thyme, sliced chilli, paprika, cumin, pepper and remaining oil in a saucepan and carefully heat over medium heat until almost boiling.

Remove the hot marinade from the heat and pour it over the fish. Cover with foil and leave to marinate for 1 hour at room temperature.

Remove the fish from the marinade and place on a serving plate. Toss the herbs with enough of the marinating liquid to coat them.

Serve the fish with the herbs sprinkled over the top and crusty bread on the side.

PAN-FRYING

Pan-frying is one of the quickest and simplest ways to prepare seafood – and one of the tastiest. The moist flesh and crisp skin provides textural contrast, while the butter or oil used to fry, plus simple seasonings such as salt, pepper and lemon juice, add great flavour.

TIPS FOR SUCCESSFUL PAN-FRYING

✳ **Be prepared before cooking.** Remove seafood from the fridge 15–30 minutes before cooking to allow it to come to room temperature. Make sure there aren't any remaining scales on the fish and pat seafood dry on a paper towel before cooking. Have garnishes, sauces and other accompaniments ready before you start cooking, so the seafood can be served as soon as it's cooked.

✳ **Arrange fillets in a single layer.** Make sure there is enough room to use a long thin fish slice (egg lifter); never use tongs as they may break delicate fillets.

✳ **Cook fillets with the skin on**. This helps to hold the flesh together and protect it from the heat of the pan. You can always peel the skin off before serving if you don't like to eat it. Cook skin-side down first for about 70 per cent of the cooking time (until the sides are opaque), then turn and cook the other side briefly to finish. Thin fillets with the skin on will sometimes curl as they begin to cook; to prevent this, press down gently using a fish slice or flat spatula until the skin starts to cook.

✳ **Remove the seafood from the heat just before it's fully cooked.** The flesh is so delicate that it will continue cooking in the residual heat.

✳ **You can finish cooking the seafood in the oven.** Chefs often pan-fry fish to brown one side, then turn it and place the pan in a 200°C (fan-forced) oven for a few minutes to finish cooking; if doing this, ensure the pan has a heatproof handle and remember that the handle will stay hot for some time after it's removed from the oven.

Recipe by
Jonathan Barthelmess

THEA DIANNE'S SALMON KEFTETHES

SERVES 6

100 ml extra virgin olive oil,
plus extra for pan-frying

1 large brown onion, finely diced

1 teaspoon ground cumin

1 teaspoon ground cinnamon

1 teaspoon ground nutmeg

2 large vine-ripened tomatoes, peeled,
seeded and finely diced, juice reserved

1½ tablespoons tomato paste (puree)

1 × 500 g piece salmon fillet, skin off,
pin-boned and finely diced

½ bunch flat-leaf parsley, leaves picked
and very finely chopped, plus extra leaves
for garnishing

½ bunch mint, leaves very finely chopped

2 tablespoons plain flour,
plus extra for rolling

salt flakes and freshly ground
white pepper, to taste

lemon cheeks, for serving

ALTERNATIVE SPECIES:
ocean trout; prawn

Jonathan Barthelmess grew up in a family of cooks and restaurateurs. He was first recognised at Coast and Manly Pavilion for his Italian-inspired cooking, but has since returned to his roots, opening Greek restaurant The Apollo. At home he sometimes cooks this seafood version of the classic Greek meatballs, keftethes, which he learnt from his Aunt Dianne. The easiest way to get the cooking time right is to cook a test one first; the trick is to have the oil hot enough to seal the patties and give them a good crust, but not so hot that the outside burns before the inside cooks. These make great finger food for a cocktail party.

Heat a frying pan over low heat and add the oil. When hot, add the onion and cook for 5–10 minutes, until it starts to caramelise. Remove from the heat and stir through the cumin, cinnamon and nutmeg. Set aside to cool.

Combine the tomato juice with ½ cup (125 ml) of water and mix in the tomato paste until smooth. Combine this with the onion, diced tomato, salmon, parsley, mint and flour. Beat well using a wooden spoon until the mixture becomes pasty and sticks together. Add salt and pepper.

Form 4 cm balls from the mixture, flatten into patties and roll in the extra flour.

Heat a frying pan over medium heat and add the oil for pan-frying. When hot, cook the patties for about 2–3 minutes each side, until just cooked through.

Serve with lemon cheeks, garnished with extra parsley leaves.

BLUE-EYE TREVALLA ON POTATO SCALES WITH SUGAR SNAP PEAS & PRESERVED LEMON

Recipe by
Stephen Hodges

It's hard to find someone more passionate about seafood than Stephen Hodges, from hole-in-the-wall café Fishface. The idea of encrusting fish with 'scales' of potato seems to have originated with French chef Paul Bocuse and has been widely taken up by chefs all over the world. Steve says that after much trial and error he settled on blue-eye trevalla as the best Australian fish for this technique; most other species give off too much liquid, which makes the potato soggy. Steve's addition of lemon agrumato and preserved lemon adds a citrus tang to this clever take on fish and chips. Agrumato oil is made by pressing citrus peel with the olives to give a subtle scent and flavour to the resulting olive oil; it's available from some delis, specialist provedores and online. You'll need a Japanese mandoline for this recipe; they're perfect for slicing vegetables very thinly – just remember they are extremely sharp so you should always use the guard.

Check the fish for any remaining scales. Cut down the bloodline of the fillet to remove the pin-bones, leaving two pieces of fish. Cut four portions from the thicker top half and two portions from the thinner belly half.

Using a Japanese mandoline, slice the potatoes as thinly as possible.

Preheat the oven to 220°C (fan-forced).

Place the fish pieces on a work surface, skin-side down. Arrange the potato slices on top of the fish in slightly overlapping layers, to resemble fish scales.

Turn the fish over onto the potato side and press down gently to ensure potato 'scales' stick. Trim around the fish to remove the excess potato.

Bring a large saucepan of salted water to the boil.

Melt the butter in an ovenproof frying pan over high heat. The butter should cover the base to a depth of 2–3 mm. When hazy, gently place the fish into the pan, potato-side down. Cook for about 1 minute, until the potato just colours, then place in the oven for 3–4 minutes, until the fish is just cooked through.

Meanwhile, blanch the sugar snap peas in the boiling salted water for 30 seconds; drain and toss with the preserved lemon and a drizzle of agrumato. Divide among six plates.

Remove the fish from the oven and return to the stovetop for a minute or so to ensure the potato scales are golden. Peel off the fish skin, then carefully turn the fish over and cook for a further 30 seconds just to seal.

Place the fish on plates, with potato scales facing up, alongside the sugar snaps. Sprinkle with salt and serve.

SERVES 6

1 × 1.5 kg blue-eye trevalla fillet, skin on

6 small desiree potatoes, peeled

300 g clarified butter (see page 89)

100 g sugar snap peas, topped and split lengthways

2 preserved lemons, rind rinsed and thinly sliced

lemon agrumato, for drizzling

salt flakes, to taste

ALTERNATIVE SPECIES:
blue warehou

SARDINIAN INVOLTINI OF JOHN DORY & PRAWNS

Giovanni Pilu loves introducing people to the produce of his native Sardinia, such as *carta di musica* – a thin, crisp, double-baked Sardinian flatbread; it's available from some delis, specialist provedores and online. In this recipe, he softens it and uses it almost like a sheet of pasta to enclose a filling of prawns and john dory before pan-frying it to re-crisp it. *Carta di musica* comes in different sizes and shapes, but it's best to use square sheets for this recipe.

In Italy, john dory is called *pesce San Pietro* (St Peter's fish) as the distinctive dark spot on either side of its body is said to be the thumb print of St Peter the fisherman. The origin of its English name is a bit hazier, though the most likely explanation is a reference to the greeny-silver hue of its skin, from *jaune doré*, French for 'golden yellow'. Regardless of what you call it, its moist flaky flesh makes it one of our finest fish. Any leftover tomato sauce is delicious tossed through pasta or served with any meat or fish.

To make the roasted tomato sauce, preheat the oven to 130°C (fan-forced). Arrange the tomatoes on a baking tray, sprinkle with salt, drizzle with a tablespoon of the oil and cook for about 30 minutes, until the skins split. Remove from the oven and increase the temperature to 200°C (fan-forced). Heat 3 tablespoons of oil in a large frying pan over medium heat and cook the garlic until soft and fragrant, being careful not to burn it. Add the tomatoes and stir to break up, then add the basil and cook for about 15 minutes, until the sauce thickens. Transfer to a blender and puree. With the motor running, drizzle in the remaining oil to emulsify. Strain the sauce through a fine sieve and keep warm.

Cut each fish fillet into three pieces lengthways, along its natural lines.

Fill a large, deep saucepan with salted water, bring to the boil, then remove from the heat. Using tongs, submerge a sheet of flatbread in the water for just a moment, then remove it and lay it flat on a clean tea towel. Repeat with the remaining carta di musica.

Stack three pieces of fish fillet on top of one another on each piece of flatbread and top each stack with 2 sage leaves and half a prawn. Sprinkle with salt and pepper and roll to form a cylinder, trimming off most of the ends and tucking the last bit in before the final roll.

Melt the butter over medium heat in a large ovenproof frying pan until foaming. Place each roll, join-side down, into the pan and cook for 30–60 seconds on each of the four sides, until golden brown all over. Place the frying pan in the oven for 3 minutes.

Remove the rolls from the pan and place on a paper towel to drain. Trim the edges and use a serrated knife to cut in half on an angle.

Spoon 2 tablespoons of the roasted tomato sauce on each plate and arrange the rolls on top. Drizzle with a little olive oil and scatter with microherbs.

Recipe by
Giovanni Pilu

SERVES 6 AS AN ENTRÉE

6 × 100 g john dory fillets, skin off

6 square sheets carta di musica (Sardinian flatbread)

12 sage leaves

3 green (raw) prawns, peeled, deveined and split lengthways

salt flakes and freshly ground black pepper, to taste

80 g salted butter

extra virgin olive oil, for drizzling

½ punnet microherbs (see Chefs' ingredients), snipped

Roasted tomato sauce

500 g truss cherry tomatoes

salt flakes, to taste

100 ml extra virgin olive oil

3 cloves garlic, finely sliced

6 basil leaves

ALTERNATIVE SPECIES:
flounder; mirror dory; sole; whiting

Recipe by
Mark Best

PAN-FRIED LEATHERJACKET
WITH TAPENADE, TOMATO & BASIL

SERVES 6

12 large vine-ripened tomatoes,
peeled, seeded and finely diced

6 spring onions (scallions),
cut into fine rings

salt flakes and freshly ground
black pepper, to taste

vegetable oil, for deep-frying

18 large basil leaves

6 × 350–450 g leatherjacket trunks,
skin off and gutted

plain flour, for dusting

100 ml extra virgin olive oil

Tapenade

250 g pitted Niçoise or Ligurian olives

50 g salted baby capers, soaked in cold
water for 1 hour, then drained and dried

1 clove garlic, roughly chopped

1 stem flat-leaf parsley, leaves picked

100 ml extra virgin olive oil

freshly ground black pepper, to taste

ALTERNATIVE SPECIES:
*garfish; john dory; mirror dory; snapper;
whiting*

Fish on the bone always has more flavour than fillets, but some people don't like looking at a fish head while they're eating. Leatherjackets are a great option as they're most commonly sold as 'trunks' (heads removed, gutted and skinned but still on the bone). They don't have many small bones to worry about either, and the moist flesh flakes easily away from the large bones. Ocean jacket is one of the most common species of leatherjacket in Australia. Mark Best tops the fish with tapenade, a Provençal olive and caper paste that is also delicious served as a dip for vegetables or on croûtons to serve with drinks.

To make the tapenade, process all ingredients in a food processor until smooth. Set aside.

Combine the tomato, spring onion, salt and pepper. Set aside.

Preheat enough vegetable oil for deep-frying in a small saucepan to 170°C (see page 61). Carefully add half the basil leaves and fry until they stop spluttering, then drain on a paper towel and sprinkle with a little salt. Repeat with remaining basil leaves. Set aside.

Preheat the oven to 60°C (fan-forced).

Rinse belly cavities of the fish with a little cold water to remove any traces of blood. Pat dry. Using a sharp knife cut three deep slits in each side of each fish. Sprinkle the fish well with salt and pepper and dust evenly with flour, shaking off any excess.

Heat a large frying pan over medium heat and add half of the olive oil. When hot, cook three of the fish for about 5–7 minutes each side, until lightly golden. Transfer the fish to a baking tray and place in the oven to keep warm. Wipe the pan clean with a paper towel and repeat with the remaining olive oil and fish.

Divide the tomato mixture among six plates and place a fish on top. Smear the tapenade over the top of each fish and garnish with basil leaves.

Recipe by
Lauren Murdoch

SKATE WITH CARAMELISED WITLOF, CAPERS & BROWN BUTTER

SERVES 6

6 × 160 g trimmed and skinned pieces skate wing

plain flour, for dusting

vegetable oil, for pan-frying

100 g unsalted butter

100 g baby capers in brine, rinsed and dried

2½ tablespoons strained lemon juice

2 tablespoons chopped flat-leaf parsley

salt flakes and freshly ground black pepper, to taste

Caramelised witlof

60 g unsalted butter, diced

40 g caster sugar

¼ teaspoon salt flakes

3 large witlof (chicory), halved lengthways

ALTERNATIVE SPECIES:
flounder; john dory

Stingray was the first recorded meal eaten by Europeans in Australia. It was cooked aboard the Endeavour in Botany Bay, which Captain Cook initially called Sting-Ray Bay. Rays and skate, like sharks, are ancient species, with skeletons made of cartilage rather than bone. Their side fins are enlarged and attached to their heads, forming a large disc-shaped 'body' with a long, thin tail. It's these enlarged side fins, called flaps or wings, that are eaten. Most fishmongers will skin and fillet the wings for you, but it's also easy to do yourself – much easier than filleting bony fish. Skate and rays are very similar, and the wings of both are generally sold as 'skate'. A great sauce for all sorts of fish, burnt butter and capers is the classic way of finishing pan-fried skate, and this dish is rarely off Lauren Murdoch's menu at Felix Bistro. The trick is to let the butter turn really brown before adding the lemon juice, which stops the cooking; otherwise you get an oily butter sauce instead of a rich nutty one. The witlof can be prepared a few hours ahead and warmed in the pan over low heat just before serving.

To make the caramelised witlof, place the butter, sugar and salt in a frying pan just large enough to hold the witlof in a single layer. Add the witlof, cut-side down, and enough water to just cover it. Press a piece of baking paper onto the surface. Bring to the boil, then reduce the heat and simmer for 10–15 minutes, until the witlof is soft. Remove the baking paper and continue cooking until the water has evaporated and the witlof has caramelised. Remove from the heat and set aside.

Dust the skate lightly with flour, shaking off any excess.

Heat a frying pan and add a little oil. Fry the skate over medium–high heat for about 2 minutes each side, depending on the thickness. Remove from the pan and keep warm.

Add the butter to the pan and heat until just brown and foaming. Add the capers and fry for 20–30 seconds, then add the lemon juice, parsley, salt and pepper.

Place one piece of witlof on each plate, top with the skate, and spoon over the caper butter. Serve immediately.

PAN-ROASTED SNAPPER WITH SWEET CORN, ZUCCHINI FLOWERS, BLACK FUNGUS & CUTTLEFISH INK

Brent Savage is an exponent of molecular gastronomy, creating clever modern food that has lively flavours and always looks great on the plate. There aren't too many chefs' tricks in this dish however, which has been on the Bentley menu since day one – just good fresh produce combined in an interesting way. Reduced veal stock is one of those ingredients chefs just happen to have on hand. It adds a rich depth to the sauce, but you could omit it and just double the amount of fish stock. Female zucchini flowers are the ones with a tiny zucchini attached to them. Cuttlefish ink is available in small sachets and jars from some fishmongers and delis; it's often called 'squid ink', but is in fact ink from cuttlefish.

To make the cuttlefish ink sauce, heat a saucepan and add the oil. When hot, add the carrot, onion, celery, garlic, bay leaves and thyme. Cook for about 5 minutes, until the onion is golden brown. Add the fish stock, bring to the boil and boil for 5–10 minutes, until reduced by half. Add the reduced veal stock, return to the boil and boil for 5–10 minutes, until reduced by half. Whisk in the cuttlefish ink, return to the boil and boil for 5–10 minutes, until the sauce has reduced to a consistency that will coat the back of a wooden spoon. Pass the sauce through a fine sieve, discarding the solids. If making in advance, set aside in the fridge.

To make the sweetcorn puree, heat a saucepan over low heat and add the oil and butter. When the butter has melted, add all of the corn kernels except for ½ cup (85 g), reserving them for later. Add the salt and cook, stirring occasionally, for 5–10 minutes, until the corn is tender. Add the milk and bring to the boil, then reduce the heat and simmer for 5–10 minutes, until the corn is very soft. Place in a blender and blend until smooth. Pass through a fine sieve and set aside, covered, to keep warm.

Remove the zucchini flower petals and soak in iced water to refresh and crisp. Dry and set them aside. Discard the stamen and cut each zucchini into four slices on the diagonal. Heat a saucepan over medium heat and add the olive oil. When hot, add the zucchini. Cook for about 1 minute, until the zucchini starts to colour and soften, then turn over. Add the black fungus and cook for a further 30 seconds. Add the reserved corn kernels and cook for a further 30 seconds. Add salt and pepper, then cover and set aside to keep warm.

Check fish for any remaining scales. Lightly score the skin and sprinkle with salt and pepper.

Heat a non-stick frying pan over medium heat and add the vegetable oil. When hot, place the fish, skin-side down, in the pan and cook for 2–3 minutes, until skin is crisp. Turn the fish over, and cook for a further 10 seconds. Add a squeeze of lemon juice, salt and pepper, then remove from the pan.

Place some sweetcorn puree in the centre of each plate and scatter some of the zucchini and fungus around the plates. Trim the ends off the fish to tidy it up and place a piece on top of the puree. Dot some cuttlefish ink sauce around the plate and garnish with the zucchini flower petals.

Recipe by
Brent Savage

SERVES 6

12 female zucchini (courgette) flowers

100 ml extra virgin olive oil

200 g black fungus, hard parts discarded, cut into bite-sized pieces

salt flakes and freshly ground white pepper, to taste

6 × 180 g pieces snapper fillet, skin on and pin-boned

1 tablespoon vegetable oil

½ lemon

Cuttlefish ink sauce

1½ tablespoons extra virgin olive oil

1 carrot, chopped

1 brown onion, chopped

1 stalk celery heart, chopped

½ head of garlic, cloves separated and peeled

3 fresh bay leaves, torn

1 bunch thyme, sprigs torn

1 cup (250 ml) Fish stock (see Basics)

1 cup (250 ml) Reduced veal stock (see Basics)

2 tablespoons cuttlefish ink

Sweetcorn puree

1 tablespoon olive oil

40 g unsalted butter

6 cobs sweetcorn, kernels removed

salt flakes, to taste

150 ml milk

ALTERNATIVE SPECIES:
blue-eye trevalla; hapuku; mulloway

Recipe by
Nino Zoccali

SEARED SWORDFISH WITH CAPONATA

SERVES 6

1 × 1.2 kg piece sashimi-grade swordfish loin, skin off and trimmed of any bloodline

salt flakes and freshly ground black pepper, to taste

1 tablespoon extra virgin olive oil

Caponata

1 tablespoon pine nuts

olive oil, for pan-frying

1 large eggplant (aubergine), finely diced

1 large red capsicum (pepper), finely diced

1 large green capsicum (pepper), finely diced

1 large yellow capsicum (pepper), finely diced

1 large red onion, finely diced

1 large stalk celery, peeled and finely diced

1 tablespoon salted baby capers, rinsed and dried

16 large green olives, pitted and finely diced

½ cup (125 ml) sweet red wine vinegar (see Chefs' ingredients)

1 tablespoon light muscovado sugar

2 teaspoons grated dark chocolate

ALTERNATIVE SPECIES:
albacore; striped marlin; tuna

Swordfish is one of the most common Mediterranean fish and is especially popular in southern Italy. Here it's teamed with caponata, a traditional Sicilian dish of sweet and sour vegetables that is enriched with a little bitter chocolate. When Nino Zoccali taught this dish at the Seafood School, he stressed that the trick to a successful caponata is to have the vegetables fried and all of the other ingredients ready so that they can be quickly combined just before serving. Italians now eat many fish just seared and still quite rare in the middle, but this is a relatively new concept and traditionally the swordfish would have been cooked all the way through, so feel free to cook it longer if that's how you like it. Nino uses vinegar made from Nebbiolo for this dish, but any sweet red wine vinegar will do.

Remove the swordfish from the fridge 30 minutes before cooking to allow it to come to room temperature.

For the caponata, place the pine nuts on a baking tray under an overhead grill and heat them, stirring frequently, until they are slightly coloured and aromatic; watch them closely as they can burn quickly. Set the toasted pine nuts aside. Heat a deep frying pan and add the oil. When hot, cook the eggplant, capsicums, onion and celery separately until just soft, adding more oil as necessary and setting each vegetable aside once cooked.

Cut the swordfish into six steaks. Sprinkle with salt and pepper.

Heat a frying pan until very hot and add the extra virgin olive oil. Add the fish and cook for a minute or so on each side; it should be warmed through but still translucent in the centre. Remove from the pan and set aside, covered, to keep warm.

Return the fried vegetables to a clean frying pan with the capers and olives and gently stir over high heat until heated through. Stir in the vinegar, sugar, chocolate and pine nuts.

Spoon the caponata onto plates and place the swordfish on top. Drizzle with a little of the dressing from the caponata, sprinkle with salt and serve.

MULLOWAY PEPERONATA

Recipe by
Peter Doyle

Peter Doyle is a master at creating colourful, tasty accompaniments that can transform a simple piece of pan-fried fish into a dinner party dish. Have a look at his romesco sauce (see page 59), which would be just as delicious in this recipe, instead of the peperonata. Master a few such accompaniments like this and you'll never be at a loss for something delicious to whip up quickly for family or friends. The amaranth, red mustard cress and baby tatsoi make a pretty combination in this dish, but use whatever microcress you can find, or even tiny leaves from a regular bunch of herbs. To make clarified butter, melt unsalted butter over low heat until the solids sink to the bottom; drain off the clear fat, discarding the solids. Ghee, which is available from some delis and supermarkets, can be substituted; it has a slightly nuttier flavour.

To make the peperonata, heat a frying pan over medium heat and add the oil. When hot, add the onion and garlic and cook, without colouring, for about 10 minutes, until soft. Add the capsicums, bay leaves, thyme, salt and pepper and increase the heat to medium–high. Cook for about 3 minutes, until the capsicum softens a little but still has some resistance. Add the tomato and cook for 2 minutes to just soften. Remove from the heat and set aside.

Preheat the oven to 230°C (fan-forced).

Check the fish for any remaining scales. Trim the belly flap and the thin edges off the fillets to neaten. Sprinkle the fish lightly with salt and pepper.

Heat the butter in a large, non-stick, ovenproof frying pan over high heat. Add the fish, skin-side down; you may need to use two pans to avoid overcrowding. Leave the fish to brown on one side for a few minutes, pressing down lightly with an egg lifter to stop it from curling. Turn over, reduce the heat and cook for another minute.

Place the pan in the oven for about 2 minutes, until the fish is almost cooked through. Remove the pan from the oven and baste the fish with a little of the cooking butter.

Combine the amaranth, red mustard microcress, baby tatsoi, dill and chervil and toss with a squeeze of lemon juice and drizzle of oil.

Place some of the peperonata on each plate and rest the fish alongside. Place a good pinch of the herb salad on top, drizzle with oil and serve with extra peperonata and lemon wedges on the side.

SERVES 6

6 × 160 g pieces mulloway fillet, skin on and pin-boned

salt flakes and freshly ground white pepper, to taste

100 ml clarified butter

1 tablespoon snipped amaranth microcress (see Chefs' ingredients)

1 tablespoon snipped red mustard microcress (see Chefs' ingredients)

1 tablespoon snipped baby tatsoi (see Chefs' ingredients)

¼ bunch dill, leaves picked

¼ bunch chervil, leaves picked

squeeze of lemon juice

extra virgin olive oil, for drizzling

lemon wedges, for serving

Peperonata

100 ml extra virgin olive oil

2 brown onions, thinly sliced

2 cloves garlic, crushed

3 red capsicums (peppers), cut into fine strips

3 yellow capsicums (peppers), cut into fine strips

2 fresh bay leaves

2 sprigs thyme

salt flakes and freshly ground white pepper, to taste

12 roma (plum) tomatoes, peeled, seeded and cut into fine strips

ALTERNATIVE SPECIES:
barramundi; bass groper; hapuku; snapper

Recipe by
Jeremy Strode

SARDINES & SOURED ONIONS ON TOAST

SERVES 6 AS AN ENTRÉE

6 thick slices sourdough bread

extra virgin olive oil,
for brushing and pan-frying

24 Australian sardines, butterflied
(see page 13), skin on and fins trimmed off

flat-leaf parsley sprigs, for garnishing

watercress sprigs, for garnishing

Soured onions

2 brown onions, very finely sliced

300 ml extra virgin olive oil

3 sprigs thyme

2 dried bay leaves

12 black peppercorns

150 ml cabernet sauvignon vinegar
(see Chefs' ingredients)

salt flakes and freshly ground
white pepper, to taste

ALTERNATIVE SPECIES:
Australian herring

Sardines are a member of the herring family, small oily fish with a distinctive 'fishy' flavour. They're popular in the United Kingdom, where Jeremy Strode grew up, and are often served with a vinegary accompaniment, like these soured onions, which cuts through their oiliness. If you haven't been a sardine fan up until now, give them a try this way. Most fishmongers sell sardines already butterflied (with the head and back bone removed, leaving the two fillets joined along the back); it's a great way to present these small fish as there aren't any bones to worry about. The soured onions will keep refrigerated for up to 2 weeks and are great with any roast meat or baked fish. Ideally start this recipe a day ahead to give the onions time to marinate.

To make the soured onions, place the onion and oil in a saucepan and cook over low heat until the onion starts to soften. Add the remaining ingredients and cook for a further 10 minutes or so, until the onion is soft. Set aside for at least 1 hour, but preferably refrigerate overnight.

Brush both sides of the bread with oil and cook on a grill or barbecue until toasted.

Check the fish for any remaining scales. Heat a non-stick frying pan over low heat and add a little oil. When hot, add the sardines, skin-side down, and cook for a minute. Turn over and cook the other side for a minute.

Place 4 sardines on top of each slice of bread and top with soured onions and their juices. Garnish with parsley and watercress sprigs and serve.

Recipe by
Armando Percuoco

BLUE-EYE TREVALLA 'ACQUA PAZZA'

SERVES 6

1 handful dried pasta (any type)

½ cup (125 ml) olive oil

4 cloves garlic, peeled

6 × 180 g pieces blue-eye trevalla fillet, skin off and pin-boned

600 g cherry tomatoes, halved

salt flakes, to taste

12 basil leaves, finely sliced

ALTERNATIVE SPECIES:
bass groper

This dish comes from Naples, as does Armando Percuoco who taught it at the Seafood School. Even Armando couldn't be certain about how the name, which means 'crazy water', came about, although it's been suggested that the water is 'crazy' because it boils so vigorously when cooking the pasta. The starch left behind in the cooking water adds a creaminess to the tomato sauce. You can use any leftover bits of pasta that you have on hand. Ensure the tomatoes are at room temperature so they don't cool the pan down too much when they're added. Some regional variations of this dish use sea water instead of the pasta cooking water.

Cook the pasta in 1.5 litres of boiling water until it is overcooked and the water is cloudy with starch. Discard the pasta and reserve 2 cups (500 ml) of the cooking water.

Heat a frying pan over medium heat and add the oil. When hot, add the garlic and cook for a couple of minutes, until golden. Add the fish and cook for 1 minute then turn over. Add the tomato. Cover the pan tightly and cook the fish for 5–10 minutes, depending on the thickness, until it is opaque almost all the way through. Remove the fish from the pan and set aside. Discard the garlic.

Add about 5 tablespoons of the pasta cooking water to the pan, or a little more if there isn't much liquid from the tomatoes. Increase the temperature and cook until the liquid is reduced to a sauce consistency, squashing the tomatoes a little with the back of a spoon or egg lifter to give a creamy consistency.

Return the fish to the pan and heat over low heat for a minute. Add the salt and most of the basil and toss well to combine.

Place the fish in the centre of the plates. Spoon the sauce over the top and garnish with the remaining basil.

Recipe by
Mark Jensen

CARAMELISED SILVER PERCH WITH SPRING ONIONS, CHILLI & BLACK PEPPER

SERVES 4

1 × 600 g silver perch, gilled, gutted and scaled

200 g white sugar

3 cloves garlic, finely chopped

2 teaspoons tomato paste

1 bunch spring onions (scallions), chopped, white and green parts separated

1 tablespoon soy sauce

3 tablespoons Vietnamese fish sauce

200 ml Fish stock (see Basics)

2 small red chillies, thinly sliced

1 teaspoon freshly cracked black pepper

steamed jasmine rice, for serving

ALTERNATIVE SPECIES:
catfish, golden perch, Murray cod, rainbow trout

Silver perch is a freshwater fish, which means it can have a slightly earthy flavour – exactly what Mark Jensen loves about this traditional dish from southern Vietnam. It's a regular on the Red Lantern menu, where this dish is cooked and served in a clay pot (available from Asian grocery stores); if you are using one, make sure it's flameproof and soaked in cold water for 30 minutes before heating. Traditionally, nothing is wasted and the fish head is cooked with the rest of the fish, but you can discard it if you prefer.

Check the fish for any remaining scales and rinse the belly cavity with a little cold water to remove any traces of blood. Pat dry. Using kitchen scissors, remove the fins and tail. Lay the fish on a chopping board and, using a large knife and working from the head towards the tail, cut the fish into 2.5 cm sections. Cut the head in half.

Combine 3 tablespoons of water and 150 g of the sugar and put into a frying pan. Place over medium heat until it is a caramel colour. Add the fish, including the head, and stir through.

Add the garlic, tomato paste and the white spring onion to the pan and cook for 1 minute, stirring constantly. Add the soy sauce, fish sauce, fish stock and half the chilli. Taste and add enough of the remaining sugar to balance the flavour to your liking. Cook for 5 minutes over low–medium heat.

Place in a serving bowl and sprinkle the pepper, remaining chilli and about 2 tablespoons of the green spring onion over the top. Serve with steamed rice.

SPAGHETTI RISOTTATI WITH SCORPIONFISH

Recipe by
Alessandro Pavoni

Cooking pasta 'in the style of a risotto' (*risottati*) means the pasta soaks up more of the flavour from the sauce as it cooks. Scorpionfish, previously called rock cod or rockfish, are very popular in the Mediterranean where they're a traditional ingredient in seafood soups. Alessandro Pavoni recommends buying whole fish and asking your fishmonger to fillet them for you so you can use the bones in the fish stock. The success of this dish relies on timing. The pasta must have been cooking for 4 minutes by the time the ingredients in the frying pan are ready for it: neither the boiled pasta nor the cooked fish can wait for one another. It's also essential to use a good artisanal durum wheat pasta that's been extruded through bronze dies, as it has a rougher surface, which the sauce clings to. Alessandro uses Fabbri brand, which is available from some delis and online.

Check the fish for any remaining scales, then dice it into 1 cm cubes.

Place the fish stock in a small saucepan and bring to the boil. Remove from the heat and cover to keep warm.

Bring a large saucepan of water to the boil. Add 3 teaspoons of salt for every litre of water. Add the spaghetti and boil for 4 minutes.

Meanwhile, heat a large frying pan over low heat and add half the oil. When hot, add the garlic, anchovies and chilli and cook for 2 minutes. Stir in the fish, and cook for 2 minutes, then remove the fish from the pan and set aside.

Add the wine to the pan, increase the heat and bring to the boil. Boil for a minute or two, until the wine evaporates, then add a ladleful of stock and return to the boil.

Drain the spaghetti and add to the frying pan. Cook, stirring constantly, for about 4 minutes, adding another ladleful of stock as each one is absorbed, until the pasta is just al dente and the sauce is creamy; you may not need all of the stock.

Remove from the heat and stir in the fish, most of the marjoram and the remaining oil. Season with salt and toss well to combine.

Serve in pasta bowls, garnished with the remaining marjoram and drizzled with oil.

SERVES 6

380 g eastern red scorpionfish fillets, skin on and pin-boned

600 ml Fish stock (see Basics)

500 g bronze-extruded spaghetti

4 tablespoons extra virgin olive oil, plus extra for drizzling

1 clove garlic, finely chopped

4 anchovy fillets in olive oil, drained and finely chopped (see Chefs' ingredients)

1 small red chilli, seeded and finely chopped

4 tablespoons dry white wine

¼ bunch marjoram, leaves picked

salt flakes, to taste

ALTERNATIVE SPECIES:
red mullet

POACHING

Poaching involves cooking food in hot liquid without boiling it; the liquid should be heated to the point where it just barely trembles. Being a gentle method that doesn't jostle the food about too much and helps retain moisture, poaching is ideal for seafood, which is relatively low in fat and has a delicate structure. Seafood is often poached in court bouillon (a vegetable stock with an acid such as lemon juice or vinegar added), stock, salted water or coconut milk (which may be flavoured with spice pastes to make curries).

TIPS FOR SUCCESSFUL POACHING

* **It's worth investing in a fish kettle** if you want to poach whole fish such as salmon.
* **When poaching fillets or small whole fish, arrange them in a single layer** to ensure even cooking.
* **Cover the pan tightly with a lid or foil** to prevent too much poaching liquid from evaporating.
* **Cook fish weighing less than 1 kg for about 1 minute per 100 g** with a minimum cooking time of 5 minutes. Add 5 minutes for each additional kilo.

STEAMING

Steaming is a quick way to cook, without the need for oil, and it keeps food moist and tasty. Built-in steamers are becoming popular in domestic kitchens, but you don't need to spend a lot of money to be able to steam food at home. A bamboo steamer ($20–30 from Asian grocery stores) that fits snugly just inside a wok or large saucepan is all you need; you can even stack two or three steamers on top of one another to cater for a crowd. Fill the wok or saucepan with enough water to come just below the base of the steamer — the simmering liquid should not touch the steamer. Wash the steamer with soapy water after each use, rinse well and leave in an airy place to dry thoroughly.

TIPS FOR SUCCESSFUL STEAMING

* **Remove seafood from the fridge 15–30 minutes before cooking** to allow it to come to room temperature. This is particularly important if fish is whole, quite thick or being served rare.
* **Place seafood on a deep plate inside the steamer.** The plate will catch any juices, and these can be poured back over the cooked seafood as a sauce. If fish is wrapped (in leaves, foil or baking paper), place it on a sheet of baking paper or banana leaves to make it easier to lift in and out of the steamer.
* **Bring the water to a simmer before placing the fish in the steamer.** Steam over medium heat, keeping the water at a simmer.
* **The steam should circulate, but not escape.** Make sure the lid and steamer are firmly in place, so that steam doesn't escape. Leave at least 1 cm between the plate, paper or leaves and the sides of the steamer, and make a few cuts in the paper or leaves to allow the steam to circulate.
* **If using a two-level steamer, swap the positions of the steamer baskets halfway through.** This will ensure even cooking.
* **Steaming cooks very quickly.** Check at the minimum cooking time, then cook a little longer if necessary. Insert a fork into the thickest part of the fish; if it's opaque all the way through and flakes easily, it's cooked. Time the cooking from when the food is placed in the steamer over simmering water and covered.
* **Beware of steam burns.** Remove the steamer from above the simmering liquid before removing the lid.

Recipe by
Neil Perry

BAR ROCK COD TAGINE

SERVES 6

1 kg bar rock cod fillet, skin off
and pin-boned

6 baby beetroots, trimmed

3 bulbs baby fennel, trimmed and quartered

12 baby carrots, trimmed

12 small kipfler potatoes

1½ cups (375 ml) Chermoula (see below)

3 tablespoons honey

1½ teaspoons salt flakes

60 g blanched almonds

80 g green olives

instant couscous, for serving

1 preserved lemon, rind rinsed and
thinly sliced

juice of 1½ lemons, strained,
more or less to taste

Chermoula

1 red onion, roughly chopped

4 cloves garlic, roughly chopped

1 bunch coriander, stalks and leaves,
roughly chopped

1 bunch flat-leaf parsley, stalks and leaves,
roughly chopped

1½ teaspoons salt flakes

1 tablespoon ground cumin

1 tablespoon ground coriander

1½ tablespoons chilli powder

1 tablespoon ground turmeric

2 teaspoons Spanish smoked sweet paprika
(see Chefs' Ingredients)

1½ tablespoons ras el hanout

185 ml extra virgin olive oil

juice of 1 lemon, strained

ALTERNATIVE SPECIES:
blue-eye trevalla; hapuku; john dory; snapper

Neil Perry is often called the father of Modern Australian cooking. He opened Rockpool in 1989, the same year Sydney Seafood School was launched, when Australia's love affair with food was in its infancy. What's become known as 'Australian' cuisine draws influences from all around the world: this dish is a good example. In Moroccan cooking, 'tagine' refers to both the cooking pot and the dish prepared in it, a slow-cooked braise or stew. Lemons preserved in salt are a delicious Moroccan ingredient: rinse them, discard the flesh and pith and use only the rind. Chermoula is a spicy herb paste often used for marinating seafood. The recipe here makes a little more than you'll need for this dish, but it keeps for up to 5 days in the fridge and is delicious with any seafood or meat; if you make it ahead of time, refrigerate until you're ready to use.

To make the chermoula, place the onion, garlic, coriander, parsley, salt, ground cumin and coriander, chilli, turmeric, paprika and ras el hanout in a food processor and process for 1 minute. With the motor running, slowly pour in the oil to form a thick paste. Stir through the lemon juice.

Cut the fish into 3–4 cm cubes. Combine the beetroot, fennel, carrot, potato, 1 litre of water, 1½ cups (375 ml) of chermoula, honey, salt, almonds and olives in a tagine or large saucepan and bring to the boil. Reduce the heat and simmer for about 1 hour, covered, until the vegetables are well cooked.

Prepare the couscous according to the packet instructions.

Stir the fish and preserved lemon through the vegetables. Simmer, uncovered, for a few minutes, until the fish is just cooked through, stirring very gently from time to time. Stir in the lemon juice and remove from the heat.

Divide among bowls or serve from the tagine or pan with the couscous on the side.

HAPUKU PROVENÇAL

Recipe by
Justin North

This rustic recipe, full of the flavours of sunny Provençe, is the sort of dish Justin North likes to cook at home for family and friends. It's particularly good for home cooking as everything goes into the one pot, meaning less washing up. Hapuku is a large coldwater fish with firm, tasty flesh that holds together well in this saucy dish. There are often a few stubborn mussels that don't open when they're cooked; use a blunt knife (such as a butter knife) to pry these open over the sink — if they look and smell good, they're fine to eat.

Sprinkle the fish with salt and pepper, and set aside in a cool place.

Heat a heavy-based, flameproof casserole dish with a tight fitting lid over medium heat and add 50 ml of the oil. When hot, add the onion, garlic, salt and pepper and cook for about 4 minutes, until the onion is translucent. Add the tomato, wine, lemon zest, olives and remaining oil and cook for about 5 minutes, until moist and pulpy.

Add the fish and mussels. Cover with the lid and cook for 3 minutes, then turn the fish and cook for about another 3 minutes, until the fish is just cooked through. As soon as each mussel opens, remove it from the pan and place it in a bowl. If the fish is cooked before all the mussels open, remove the fish from the pan, then cover the pan, shake it well and cook for a further couple of minutes until the remaining mussels open.

Return the mussels and fish to the pan, then add salt, pepper and basil leaves and serve with crusty bread.

SERVES 6

6 × 160 g pieces hapuku fillet, skin off, pin-boned and bloodline removed

salt flakes and freshly ground white pepper, to taste

200 ml extra virgin olive oil

1 red onion, thinly sliced

6 cloves garlic, thinly sliced

8 very ripe tomatoes, chopped

150 ml dry white wine

finely grated zest of 1 lemon

½ cup (60 g) pitted green olives

24 blue mussels, scrubbed and debearded (see page 121)

1 handful basil leaves, torn

crusty bread, for serving

ALTERNATIVE SPECIES:
bar rock cod; bass groper; blue-eye trevalla; leatherjacket; Murray cod

Recipe by
Ajoy Joshi

BREAM IN GREEN CHATNI STEAMED IN BANANA LEAVES

SERVES 6

3 banana leaves, wiped with a clean, damp cloth on both sides

12 × 90 g bream fillets, skin off and pin-boned

3 large vine-ripened tomatoes, cut into wedges

2 lemons, cut into wedges

salt flakes and freshly ground black pepper, to taste

steamed basmati rice, for serving

Chatni

1 coconut, grated

3 small green chillies, chopped

3 long green chillies, chopped

½ bunch coriander, leaves picked

½ bunch mint, leaves picked

2.5 cm piece ginger, roughly chopped

2 cloves garlic, roughly chopped

½ teaspoon ground turmeric

1 teaspoon cumin seeds

juice of 2 lemons, strained

salt flakes, to taste

¼ teaspoon white sugar

3 tablespoons vegetable oil

ALTERNATIVE SPECIES:
barramundi; flathead; snapper

Ajoy Joshi loves to share India's diverse regional and ethnic cuisines with his restaurant guests and cooking class attendees. This classic Parsi dish from north-western India, called *Patra ni Machchi*, uses a spicy green *chatni* (the Indian name for a fresh relish, from which the English word 'chutney' is derived). It adds great flavour to any fish. Wrapping fish in banana leaves before cooking helps to keep it moist. The leaves are quickly seared first to help them retain their colour. In Indian culture, banana leaves represent purity and so food is often served on them as a sign of freshness. You'll need toothpicks or kitchen string to hold the banana leaf parcels together, and you may need to use two steamer baskets stacked on top of one another to hold the six parcels.

To make the chatni, place all the ingredients except the oil in a food processor and process to combine. With the motor running, slowly pour in the oil to make a thick paste. Taste and add more salt if needed. Set aside.

Remove any stem sections from the banana leaves, then cut six large squares of banana leaf, each large enough to completely enclose a fillet. Heat a large frying pan and place each square of banana leaf, shiny-side down, in the pan for a few seconds to just singe. Lay the banana leaves on a work surface, singed-side up.

Spread half the chatni all over the fillets. Place two fillets on top of each other on each piece of banana leaf. Reserve the remaining chatni to serve as a sauce. Wrap the banana leaves around the fillets to form parcels, sealing them securely with toothpicks or kitchen string.

Place the parcels in a large steamer and steam for 10–12 minutes, until the flesh flakes easily when tested with a fork.

Meanwhile, dress the tomatoes with a squeeze of lemon juice, salt and pepper.

Place the fish parcels on plates for diners to open at the table, with a lemon wedge on the side. Serve with the remaining chatni, tomatoes and steamed rice.

Recipe by
Kylie Kwong

STEAMED WHOLE CORAL TROUT WITH GINGER & SPRING ONIONS

SERVES 4

1 × 700–800 g coral trout, gilled, gutted and scaled

3 tablespoons shao hsing

1 × 30 g (4 cm) piece ginger, cut into fine matchsticks

3 tablespoons tamari

½ teaspoon sesame oil

1 teaspoon white sugar

4 spring onion (scallions), cut into fine matchsticks

3 tablespoons peanut oil

1 small handful coriander leaves

pinch of ground white pepper

steamed jasmine rice, for serving

ALTERNATIVE SPECIES:
barramundi; King George whiting; pigfish; snapper

Kylie Kwong taught this classic Chinese dish at the Seafood School many years ago, when she was still at Wockpool. It's a great example of how simply seafood can be prepared – as long as you start with the freshest produce, you don't need to do much to it. Coral trout, with its bright red skin and distinctive blue spots, is a beautiful fish to serve whole. In this dish, the sugar balances the saltiness of the tamari, while sesame oil adds an extra flavour dimension and the hot peanut oil releases the aromas of the ginger and onions and marries all the elements together. Add some steamed or stir-fried Asian greens to round out the meal. Shao hsing is a Chinese cooking wine; it's widely available from Asian grocers.

Check the fish for any remaining scales and rinse the belly cavity with a little cold water to remove any traces of blood. Pat dry. Place the fish on a chopping board. Using kitchen scissors, trim the tail if necessary so that the fish will fit inside the steamer with the lid firmly closed. Using a sharp knife, make four diagonal slits into one side of the fish through to the bone, then repeat in the opposite direction to make a diamond pattern. Turn the fish over and repeat on the other side.

Bring a deep saucepan or wok of water to the boil. Place the fish on a heatproof plate that will fit inside a steamer basket. Pour 4 tablespoons of water and the shao hsing over the fish and sprinkle with half the ginger. Place the plate inside the steamer and set over the saucepan or wok. Cover and steam for 8–10 minutes, until the flesh is opaque through to the bone; if it's still translucent, cook for another minute or so.

Combine the tamari and sesame oil. Using two spatulas or egg lifters, carefully remove the fish from the steamer and place it on a serving plate. Pour any liquid left in the dish over the fish, sprinkle with sugar and drizzle with the combined tamari and sesame oil. Sprinkle with the remaining ginger and half the spring onion.

Heat the peanut oil in a small saucepan until smoking, then carefully pour over the fish. Sprinkle with the remaining spring onion, coriander and pepper, and serve immediately with steamed rice.

STEAMED MURRAY COD ROLLS

Chui Lee Luk has a delicate hand with seafood, always cooking it so that it remains beautifully moist, and enhancing it with subtle flavours that don't overpower it. Murray cod, a native Australian freshwater fish, has lovely firm white flesh, which looks beautiful against the bright green spring onions, and a delicate flavour that marries well with the slightly smoky dashi stock. It's important that the pieces of fish are a uniform size and thickness so they will form a neat parcel and cook evenly. For this reason, don't buy fillets that may well come from different fish; instead, buy a whole fish and ask your fishmonger to fillet and skin it for you. The roll can be prepared up to the refrigeration stage and kept overnight, ready to steam and serve the next day, making it perfect for a large group. You can also make a more substantial entrée for six by serving two pieces of roll per person.

To make the dashi stock, bring the chicken stock to the boil. Remove the pan from the heat, scatter the bonito over the top, and set aside to steep for 10 minutes. Strain the stock into a clean saucepan, then stir in the soy sauce, mirin and pepper. Cover and set aside.

Starting at the head end of the fish, cut one fillet lengthways along the central pin-bones until you reach the end of the bones, then cut upwards to remove the thicker upper portion, leaving the tail section attached to the belly piece. Cut along the other side of the bones and discard the central strip with the bones. Butterfly the upper portion by slicing horizontally almost all of the way through (from the longer side), then opening it out to form a rough rectangle. Set aside, then repeat with the other fillet. Finally, lay the two tail sections side by side, head to tail. Trim to make a rectangular shape, then slice the trimmings horizontally and lay them over the thinner sections to give a roughly even thickness. Cover and refrigerate the three rectangles of fish until needed.

Preheat the oven to 150°C (fan-forced). Toast the nori on a baking tray for about 5 minutes, until brittle. Slice into fine strips and set aside.

Trim the spring onions to the length of the fish rectangles. Heat a frying pan over high heat, drizzle in a little olive oil and sprinkle in some salt. Add the spring onions and fry them for a few minutes, until they are bright green and slightly charred. Refrigerate to cool.

Lay two sheets of plastic wrap on a work surface, slightly overlapping. Scatter with a third of the nori, then place a rectangle of fish on top. Sprinkle with sugar, salt and pepper, then squeeze the ginger over the fish to extract some of its juice. Lay 3 spring onions and a third of the crab meat along the centre of the fish. Roll up tightly into a sausage shape, twisting the ends of the plastic wrap and tucking them under to secure. Repeat with the remaining ingredients to make three rolls in total, then refrigerate the rolls for a couple of hours or overnight.

Meanwhile, blanch the broccolini in boiling salted water for 3 minutes, until just tender. Drain and refresh in iced water, then drain again.

Steam the rolls over barely simmering water for 15–20 minutes, until the fish is just opaque, adding the broccolini to the steamer in the last couple of minutes to warm.

Meanwhile, reheat the dashi stock over low heat.

Cut each roll into four portions, then remove the plastic wrap gently from each portion. Place a piece of roll in each of twelve soup bowls along with the broccolini. Pour the hot dashi stock over the top and serve.

Recipe by
Chui Lee Luk

SERVES 12 AS AN ENTRÉE

1 × 1–1.5 kg Murray cod, filleted and skinned

2 sheets nori

9 spring onions (scallions), peeled

extra virgin olive oil, for pan-frying

salt flakes and freshly ground white pepper, to taste

½ teaspoon caster sugar

5 cm piece ginger, peeled and pounded to form a paste

50 g cooked crabmeat, checked for cartilage and well drained (see page 179)

12 stems broccolini, cut into florets and stems peeled and sliced

Dashi stock

800 ml Chicken stock (see Basics)

10 tablespoons (10 g) shaved bonito flakes

3 tablespoons soy sauce, more or less, to taste

2 tablespoons mirin, more or less, to taste

freshly ground white pepper, to taste

ALTERNATIVE SPECIES:
barramundi; King George whiting; mulloway

Recipe by
Guillaume Brahimi

BOUILLABAISSE

SERVES 6 AS AN ENTRÉE

1 kg mixed small white fish (such as flathead, leatherjacket, red gurnard, red mullet, scorpionfish and whiting), gilled, gutted and scaled

2 tablespoons extra virgin olive oil, plus extra for pan-frying

2 cloves garlic

1 bulb fennel, trimmed and diced

2 leeks, white part only, washed and diced

2 brown onions, diced

1 bouquet garni

2 tablespoons tomato paste

8 vine-ripened tomatoes, diced

large pinch of saffron threads

cayenne pepper, to taste

18 thin slices baguette

salt flakes, to taste

rind of 2 oranges, in large strips

1 bunch French tarragon (see Chefs' ingredients), leaves picked and chopped

6 green (raw) prawns, peeled and deveined (see page 181)

2 × 150 g john dory fillets, skin off, each cut into 3 pieces

Aïoli (see Basics), for serving

½ bunch chives, finely snipped

ALTERNATIVE SPECIES:
*snapper (instead of john dory);
scallop (instead of prawn)*

Seafood soups are made all over the Mediterranean, traditionally by fishermen cooking whatever they couldn't sell from the day's catch in a large cauldron over an open fire on the beach. Scorpionfish (previously called rock cod or rockfish) are one of the most common ingredients. The more varieties of fish, the greater the flavour: a traditional bouillabaisse calls for at least half a dozen species; saffron and dried orange peel are also essential ingredients. Guillaume Brahimi's refined version extracts plenty of flavour from the small bony fish, which are then discarded, and a luxurious touch is added with pan-fried john dory and prawns. Make a bouquet garni by tying a stem of coriander, a stem of flat-leaf parsley and a bay leaf together with some kitchen string. You'll need a mouli food mill to make this dish.

Check the whole fish for any remaining scales. Rinse the belly cavities with a little cold water to remove any traces of blood. Chop each fish into four or five pieces.

Heat a large, deep frying pan over medium heat and add the 2 tablespoons of oil. When hot, add the garlic, fennel, leek, onion, bouquet garni and pieces of fish, then reduce the heat to low and cook, without browning, for 8 minutes. Add the tomato paste, tomato, 1.5 litres of water, saffron and cayenne pepper. Cover and bring to the boil, then reduce the heat and simmer for 45 minutes.

Meanwhile, arrange the baguette slices on a baking tray and place under a hot grill for a few minutes on each side until crisp and lightly golden.

Remove the bouquet garni from the pan and place the fish, vegetables and cooking liquid in a blender and roughly blend. Pass through a mouli food mill, then through a fine sieve, pressing down to extract as much liquid as possible. Discard the solids.

Return the liquid to a clean saucepan and bring to a very gentle simmer. Add the salt, orange rind and tarragon and cook for a few minutes to warm through. Taste and add more salt and cayenne if needed. Remove the orange rind and blitz the soup using a stick blender.

Heat a frying pan and add a little oil. When hot, cook the prawns and john dory for a minute or two each side, until just cooked through. Divide the prawns and fish among warmed soup bowls, spoon the soup over and place an aïoli-topped croûton in each bowl. Sprinkle with chives. Serve the remaining aïoli and croûtons separately.

SHELL

UNIVALVES & BIVALVES

Univalves, also called gastropods, are creatures that live inside one shell, such as abalone. For our purposes here, we're also including sea urchins, although technically they belong to a different class of animal. Bivalves, as the name suggests, are two-shelled creatures such as oysters, scallops, mussels, clams and pipis.

ABALONE

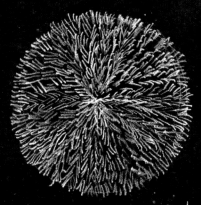

SEA URCHIN

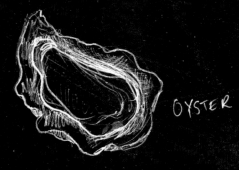

OYSTER

ABALONES

Univalves aren't generally popular eating, but the 100 or so species of abalone found around the world are the exception. They live in the swell zone along open coastlines and so have developed a large muscular foot with which they firmly attach themselves to their rocky homes. This firm muscle is the part that is eaten. Australia has two main abalone species, greenlip and blacklip, differentiated by the colour of the dark lip around the edge of their foot. Some are harvested from the wild and some are farmed; small farmed greenlip abalones are sold as cocktail abalones.

SEA URCHINS

Sea urchins have round, spiny shells that are divided internally into five chambers. Each chamber contains an orange roe, which is the part that is eaten.

OYSTERS

Oysters have been eaten for at least 30,000 years. A prized food in Roman times, and a food of the poor in Medieval England, they are now the most esteemed molluscs worldwide. Australia has three food oysters: Sydney rocks, Pacifics and natives (previously called angasis). Flavour varies significantly depending on the environment in which the oyster grows, so there's a great diversity of tastes available. Native oysters, large, flat, meaty oysters native to the southern coast of Australia, aren't as common as Pacific or Sydney rock oysters, but they are worth looking out for.

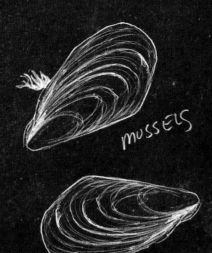

MUSSELS

COMMERCIAL SCALLOP

VONGOLE

SURF CLAM

MUSSELS

Once popular as snacks that could be harvested free or purchased cheaply (and known as 'poor man's oysters'), mussels are still one of the most affordable shellfish available. Australian mussels are called blue mussels due to the dark blue, almost black, colour of their shell. New Zealand green mussels, while delicious in New Zealand where they're available fresh, are par-cooked before being exported to Australia to satisfy quarantine requirements; this initial cooking means they toughen up if recooked, so they aren't a suitable alternative to blue mussels.

CLAMS

Vongole, meaning clams in Italian, is the name given to Australia's most common clams. They have small, oval shells with concentric ridges and bury themselves in sand around the southern coast of Australia. There are a number of different kinds, with shells ranging from white to light brown in colour, sometimes with darker zigzag markings. Surf clams are larger than vongole. Their rough, circular shells have sculpted, concentric ridges, often with darker patterning; they vary from cream to light brown. We're starting to see a wider range of clams in Australia, including the strawberry cockle and blood cockle.

SAUCER SCALLOP

SCALLOPS

Australia has two main species of scallop: commercial and saucer. Commercial scallops (previously called Tasmanian, king or sea scallops) have creamy-coloured flesh and are generally sold with their orange roe attached; the ridged, oval shell is a pale pink–red colour. Saucer scallops (previously called Queensland, white or mud scallops) have firmer, whiter flesh and are generally sold roe-off, often still attached to their almost round, smooth reddish-brown shell.

PIPIS

PIPIS

Pipis, which are closely related to clams, are found all around the Australian coast, again buried in sand. They are larger than vongole and their smooth, wedge-shaped shells are cream to pale brown, sometimes tinged with purple. As the most common sizeable mollusc found along ocean beaches in New South Wales, they constituted an important food source for indigenous Australians for thousands of years, as is evidenced by the many middens of pipi shells left behind.

117

CHOOSING, STORING & COOKING UNIVALVES & BIVALVES

UNIVALVES

 Abalone is available in the shell (live or frozen), or as meat (frozen and vacuum-packed, or dried). Farmed 'cocktail' abalone is generally less expensive than abalone harvested from the wild. Abalone is best bought live from a tank.

Sea urchin roe is available in small wooden or plastic boxes from good fishmongers and doesn't require any trimming or preparation. Live sea urchins usually need to be pre-ordered. If you do buy a live sea urchin, chef Janni Kyritsis suggests this simple way of opening it: cut a small hole in the top, where the mouth is, then place the tips of a pair of pliers into the hole and, using two hands, pull the pliers apart to crack the shell open. This will reveal two sections, one with two pieces of roe and one with three pieces.

 Live abalone can be kept for up to 3 days stored in a deep-sided bucket covered with a damp cloth and stored in the coolest part of the house. Refrigerate abalone meat for 2–3 days.

Store live sea urchins in the warmest part of the fridge (usually the crisper) for up to 4 days covered with a cloth that is kept damp. Store fresh roe that you've extracted from live sea urchins in a container covered with a solution made from 10 g salt and 1 litre of water for up to 2 days, but it's best served as soon as it's extracted from the shell. Boxed roe can be stored in the fridge for up to a few days.

BIVALVES

When choosing bivalves, look for:

- brightly coloured, lustrous shells;
- intact shells that are closed, or close when tapped or gently squeezed;
- a pleasant fresh sea smell.

Ideally, learn to shuck your own oysters (see page 121), or at least buy them freshly shucked and not washed.

Scallops are one of the few bivalves not generally sold live, though chefs often prefer to buy them live and shuck them themselves. Raw scallops should be translucent and slightly 'sticky', indicating that they haven't been frozen or stored in water (scallop meat is sponge-like and will quickly absorb water, turning opaque).

 Store unopened oysters in the warmest part of the fridge (usually the crisper) for up to a week, covered with a cloth that is kept damp. Once opened, store oysters in the fridge with a damp cloth covering them and eat them as soon as possible, certainly the same day if raw or within 24 hours if cooking them.

To store scallop meat, place it on a plate, cover with plastic wrap and refrigerate for up to 3 days. Live scallops should be consumed as soon as possible after purchase; store in a container, covered with a cloth that is kept damp, in the warmest part of the fridge (usually the crisper).

Mussels, clams and pipis are sold live and should be eaten as soon as possible. They can be stored overnight, covered with a cloth that is kept damp, in the warmest part of the fridge (usually the crisper).

 Bivalves that live in a sandy environment, such as vongole, surf clams and pipis, need to be purged to remove the sand before cooking. They're usually sold already purged, but it doesn't hurt to place them in a solution of cool water and sea salt (30 g salt to each litre of water) for several hours, or overnight, before cooking them. Store them in a cool place, but don't refrigerate them or they'll close up and won't 'spit out' the sand. Mussels don't need to be purged as they grow on ropes suspended in the water.

Before cooking live bivalves, discard any shells that are open and don't close when tapped or gently squeezed (you may need to give them 10–20 minutes out of the fridge to warm up first).

When cooking live bivalves, it's best to remove them from the pan with tongs as each shell opens, so as not to overcook them. There are often a few stubborn shells that don't open when they're cooked; use a blunt knife (such as a butter knife) to pry these open over the sink and if they look and smell good, they are fine to eat.

PREPARING ABALONE

1 Slide a short-bladed knife around the edge of the abalone, between the meat and the shell.

2 Turn the meat over.

3 Cut off and discard the intestine (the small sac attached to the underside). Rinse and dry the meat.

4 Cut off and discard the small piece of gristle at the head end (next to the small antennae).

5 Trim off and discard the lip and frill.

6 Cut a thin layer off the surface of the abalone foot (where it attached to the rock). Discard.

7 Using a small paring knife, scrape away any dark parts.

8 Under cold running water, use a small paring knife to scrape off the brown film remaining on the sides. The frill and lip don't need to be trimmed off cocktail abalone, but the dark film still needs to be scraped off the foot and the sides to prevent it becoming tough.

SHUCKING OYSTERS

1 Rinse the oysters under cold water to remove any excess dirt. Fold a tea towel around the wide end of the oyster shell and rest it on a chopping board, flat-side up, with the narrow end pointing out.

2 Insert the tip of an oyster knife (see Seafood kit) between the top and bottom shell at the narrow end; twist to pop the shell open. Cut through the muscle attaching the oyster to the top shell; remove and discard this shell.

3 Carefully run the knife underneath the oyster to remove it from the bottom shell. Flip the oyster over for presentation, if you like.

TRIMMING SHUCKED SCALLOPS

SCRUBBING & DEBEARDING MUSSELS

1 Trim off the small dark vein that runs along the side.

1 Scrub two mussels together under cold running water to remove any barnacles from the shell.

2 Hold the shell firmly closed and tug sharply on the 'beard', pulling it away from the pointy end of the shell. Alternatively, cook mussels with the beards on and remove them once the shells have opened.

STEAMED ABALONE CUSTARD WITH POACHED CHICKEN SALAD

Phillip Searle was one of the first chefs to introduce Asian flavours into Australian fine dining at his highly acclaimed Oasis Seros in the late 1980s. He taught this dish at the Seafood School in 1991, when fresh abalone wasn't widely available and he wanted to distil the flavour from frozen abalone; back then he discarded the abalone after the stock was made. Thankfully today the long, slow cooking of fresh abalone produces a delicately flavoured stock plus delicious abalone slices to toss through the salad. This method of 'steam simmering' by enclosing the abalone in a well-sealed bowl inside a well-sealed dish is a classic Japanese technique. It's worth noting that 3 parts stock to 1 part eggs will work for any savoury custard. You'll need only half the chicken for this recipe; keep the leftovers for another dish.

Pull out and discard excess fat from the chicken cavity, then rinse to remove any traces of blood. Place the chicken in a saucepan just large enough to hold it. Add the spring onions and ginger and cover with cold water. Bring to the boil, then reduce the heat and skim to remove any froth that floats to the top. Simmer for 30 minutes, skimming occasionally. Remove the saucepan from the heat, then cover and set aside to steep for 1 hour.

Remove the chicken from the cooking liquid and place it in iced water until cold. Strain the chicken stock and set it aside. Drain the chicken, pat it dry and set it aside (don't refrigerate unless preparing in advance).

Preheat the oven to 180°C (fan-forced). Place the abalone in a stainless-steel bowl with a lip and add 2 litres of the chicken stock. Place a sheet of baking paper on the surface of the stock and cover the bowl with foil, crimping underneath the lip of the bowl to seal tightly.

Place the bowl in a deep, lidded baking dish and add boiling water to come halfway up the side of the bowl. Cover the dish with a tight-fitting lid and place in the oven for 3 hours.

Remove the dish from the oven and increase the oven temperature to 200°C (fan-forced). Remove the lid and foil from the dish and set it aside to cool a little.

Remove the abalone from the stock, reserving the stock, and set it aside at room temperature to cool. Very finely slice the abalone, cover it and set it aside at room temperature.

Pass the abalone stock through a fine sieve and measure 1.8 litres. Set the stock aside to come to room temperature, then add salt. Meanwhile, boil the remaining abalone stock until reduced to about 2½ tablespoons. Set this aside to use in the dressing.

Gently beat the eggs in a bowl, without making them frothy, while pouring in the 1.8 litres of abalone stock in a thin stream. Pass this through a fine sieve.

Place a tea towel, folded in half, in the bottom of a baking dish. Place eight 300 ml-capacity ovenproof bowls on the tea towel and ladle the egg mixture into them. Pour boiling water into the baking dish to come halfway up the sides of the bowls. Place in the oven and cook for about 30 minutes, until the custards are just set; the surface should still wobble. Remove from the oven and set aside in the water bath to cool.

Combine the mirin, soy sauce, sesame oil, reduced abalone stock, salt and pepper to make a dressing.

Tear half the chicken breast meat into fine strips, following the muscle structure.

Place the shredded chicken in a bowl with the abalone, watercress, mizuna and the dressing and toss gently. Place the custards on plates with the salad alongside and serve warm.

Recipe by
Phillip Searle

SERVES 6 AS AN ENTRÉE

1 × 1.5–2 kg free-range chicken

4 spring onions (scallions), roughly chopped

1 tablespoon chopped ginger

3 abalone, cleaned (see page 120)

salt flakes and freshly ground black pepper, to taste

10 × 55 g eggs

2 tablespoons mirin

2 tablespoons light soy sauce

2 drops of sesame oil

1 handful watercress sprigs

1 handful red and green mizuna

ALTERNATIVE SPECIES:
none

Recipe by
Janni Kyritsis

SEA URCHIN SANDWICHES

MAKES 18 SMALL FINGER SANDWICHES

50 g salted butter, softened

finely grated zest of 1 lemon

6 slices white sandwich bread

3 live sea urchins (see page 119)
or 15 sea urchin roe

ALTERNATIVE SPECIES:
none

The Greeks have enjoyed sea urchins since ancient times, so who better to give us a quick and delicious way to prepare them than Janni Kyritsis? Lee Hokianga, Janni's chef at MG Garage Restaurant, introduced him to this way of serving the spiny creatures. She had fond memories of collecting them on the beach with her Maori father, who simply removed the roe there and then and served them to his children on buttered white bread. At MG Garage, Janni also served the split urchin shells simply on a bed of seaweed and crushed ice.

Combine the butter and lemon zest. Spread over one side of each slice of bread. Divide the roe among 3 slices of bread and top with the remaining slices of bread.

Cut off the crusts, slice each sandwich in half lengthways, then slice each half in thirds crossways to make six small fingers from each sandwich.

Recipe by
George Francisco

SYDNEY ROCK OYSTERS WITH FIRE ICE

SERVES 6 AS AN ENTRÉE

36 Sydney rock oysters, freshly shucked (see page 121), on the half shell

rock salt or crushed ice, for serving

Fire ice

300 ml cold water

5 teaspoons sambal oelek (chilli paste)

5 teaspoons caster sugar

2 teaspoons fish sauce (see Chefs' ingredients)

ALTERNATIVE SPECIES:
native oyster; Pacific oyster

It's hard to find original things to do with raw oysters, and while a squeeze of lemon juice or splash of Tabasco sauce is often all they need, it's sometimes fun to dress them up a little. George Francisco is passionate about fresh oysters and recommends learning to shuck them yourself, so that you can open them just before serving. He created fire ice when he worked at Farallon in San Francisco and brought it to Australia with him, serving it at Jonah's at Whale Beach. It's basically a slightly sweet, slightly hot, slightly salty granita, and its icy texture contrasts beautifully with creamy oysters. It keeps, frozen, for 2–3 weeks and just needs to be scraped with a fork before serving. Sambal oelek is an Asian paste of salt and chillies; it adds a great kick without being too hot.

To make the fire ice, place all the ingredients in a large bowl and whisk together until the sugar has dissolved. Transfer to a large shallow metal tin or dish and place in the freezer, ensuring it is level. Every 15 minutes or so, scrape the mixture with a fork; as the liquid freezes, the scraping will create ice crystals, giving a granita texture.

Arrange the oysters on a plate lined with rock salt or crushed ice. Place a teaspoon of fire ice on top of each oyster and serve immediately.

Recipe by
Peter Gilmore

PACIFIC OYSTERS WITH DASHI JELLY

SERVES 6 AS AN ENTRÉE

18 Pacific oysters, freshly shucked
(see page 121), on the half shell

rock salt or crushed iced, for serving

Dashi jelly

10 cm strip (5 g) kombu (dried kelp)

2 cups (500 ml) water

1 cup lightly packed (12 g) shaved
bonito flakes

3 sheets gold-grade leaf gelatine

2 tablespoons salt-reduced soy sauce

25 ml mirin

ALTERNATIVE SPECIES:
native oyster; Sydney rock oyster

Peter Gilmore taught this recipe in an oyster workshop he conducted at the Seafood School. The smokiness of the dashi jelly marries beautifully with the slightly sweet, briny oysters. Leaf gelatine is available from delis and specialist provedores in various grades (silver, gold or titanium), each with a different setting strength; if gold is unavailable, ask the retailer for advice on the quantity of another grade to use. Chefs generally prefer leaf to powdered gelatine as it gives a smoother, clearer jelly, but you could substitute 5 g of powdered gelatine in this recipe if leaf gelatine is unavailable. If you're in a hurry you can speed up the setting process by placing the jelly in a metal bowl over a larger bowl containing an ice slurry (crushed ice and water).

Place the kombu and water in a non-reactive saucepan and bring to almost boiling point, but do not allow it to boil. Remove from the heat and discard the kombu.

While the water is still hot, scatter the bonito over the top and set the dashi stock aside to infuse for 20 minutes–1 hour.

Pass the dashi through a fine sieve into a clean saucepan, discarding the bonito flakes (do not press the flakes to extract the liquid as this will make the dashi cloudy). Bring the dashi to the boil, then remove it from the heat immediately.

Soak the gelatine in a little cold water, then gently squeeze out the liquid. Add the softened gelatine to the dashi with the soy sauce and mirin. Stir gently until the gelatine has completely dissolved.

Pour the dashi into a container to a depth of about 2 cm. Refrigerate for at least 2 hours, until the jelly is lightly set.

Using a teaspoon, gently chop the jelly into small pieces. Spoon it onto the oysters and serve immediately on a bed of rock salt or crushed ice.

Recipe by
Guillaume Brahimi

GENTLY BAKED NATIVE OYSTERS WITH CURRY BUTTER

SERVES 6 AS AN APPETISER

120 g salted butter, softened

rock salt, for cooking and serving

6 native (angasi) oysters, freshly shucked (see page 121), on the half shell

Curry powder

40 g coriander seeds (about ½ cup)

20 g cumin seeds (about 4 tablespoons)

15 g fenugreek seeds (about 3 teaspoons)

15 g yellow mustard seeds (about 3 teaspoons)

5 g fennel seeds (about 3 teaspoons)

5 g cinnamon quill (about 1 small quill)

6 green cardamom pods, seeds only

3 cloves

10 g ground turmeric (about 1 tablespoon)

ALTERNATIVE SPECIES:
large Pacific oyster; blue mussel

This dish was on the menu at Guillaume at Bennelong in 2001, when the restaurant had just opened. Large, flat native oysters (previously known as angasi oysters) are related to the famed Belon oyster of northern France. In this recipe, they are heated just long enough to melt the butter, leaving them plump and juicy. The curry powder recipe makes more than you'll need for this dish, but is hard to make in smaller quantities. Store leftovers in an airtight container in a cool, dry place for up to a month and use for seafood curry.

To make the curry powder, place all the ingredients except the turmeric in a frying pan over low heat and cook for a few minutes, until fragrant. Place in a mortar and grind to a powder with a pestle. Pass through a fine sieve, then stir in the turmeric.

Preheat the oven to 160°C (fan-forced). Combine the butter and 2 tablespoons of the curry powder, mix well and set aside. Place rock salt on a baking tray and rest the oysters on top. Cover each oyster with butter, then bake for about 6 minutes, until the butter is melted and warm.

Serve the oysters on a bed of rock salt.

CHILLED VICHYSSOISE WITH OYSTER BEIGNETS

They say that chefs don't choose signature dishes, diners do. Dietmar Sawyere regularly changes the menu at Berowra Waters Inn, but hasn't been able to take this dish off the menu since he opened because returning guests request it, and new ones have heard about it and want to try it. You'll need an old-fashioned, chargeable whipped cream siphon to make this dish (if you happen to have two, it's even easier, as you can chill the beignet batter in one and the vichyssoise in the other!). You can buy them, and the charges for them, from kitchenware stores or online (it's important to buy cream charges not soda ones for this recipe). If you don't have one, you can omit the gelatine and froth the cold vichyssoise with a stick blender, though it won't have the same light, mousse-like texture; the batter can be used without foaming if necessary. Vichyssoise is a classic cold potato and leek soup, which has a natural affinity for the briny flavour of oysters. Any leftover vichyssoise can be heated and served as a hot soup. Oscietra caviar gives this dish a decadent touch, but you can leave it out and use a little extra salmon roe if you prefer. You could also use small ramekins instead of demitasse or Chinese tea cups. You'll need to start this recipe a day ahead to make the batter.

To make the beignet batter, sift the plain flour, rice flour and baking powder together. Dissolve the honey in the vodka and add to the flour mixture, mixing to make a dough. Cover and refrigerate overnight.

The next day, mix the beer into the dough, and chill for 1 hour.

For the vichyssoise, melt the butter in a saucepan, add the onion and leek, and cook, covered, over low heat for 8–10 minutes, until tender but not coloured. Meanwhile, bring the chicken stock to a simmer in a saucepan. Stir the potatoes and oyster sauce into the leek mixture. Add the chicken stock and bring to the boil, then reduce the heat and simmer for about 15 minutes, until the potatoes start to break down. Stir in the cream, return to the boil and cook for a couple of minutes, then set aside for 15 minutes to cool. Taste and add salt if necessary. Add the gelatine and stir until dissolved. Place the soup in a blender and blend until very smooth, then cover and refrigerate for a few hours until set. Spoon the vichyssoise into the canister of a chargeable whipped cream siphon and charge with two cream gas cartridges. Shake well and chill for 30 minutes before using.

Preheat the oven to 200°C (fan-forced). Heat the clarified butter in a small saucepan, add the bread and fry until golden brown. Drain on paper towel, sprinkle with salt and set aside. Melt the unsalted butter in a frying pan, add the leek and cook, covered, for 8–10 minutes, until tender but not coloured. Add the wine and cook until it evaporates, then stir in the cream and salt. Cook over low heat for about 10 minutes, until the leeks are soft and the cream has reduced by about three-quarters.

Meanwhile, remove the oysters from their shells and place the oyster shells in the oven for about 5 minutes to warm.

Preheat the oil to 250°C. Remove the oyster shells from the oven and turn it off. Divide the leek mixture among the shells and return them to the oven to keep warm. Half-fill six demitasse or Chinese tea cups with the foamed vichyssoise and divide the caviar and roe among the cups. Fill with more foamed vichyssoise and sprinkle the top with croûtons and chives.

Place the cups of vichyssoise on plates with a small mound of rock salt beside each one. Rinse the cream canister (unless you have a spare), then spoon in the beignet batter and charge with three cream gas cartridges. Dust the oysters lightly in rice flour, shaking off any excess. Squirt some beignet batter into a small bowl and dip the oysters into it, then carefully lower them into the oil and deep-fry for 30–40 seconds, until golden brown. Drain on paper towel. Place the oysters on top of the leek in the oyster shells and place 2 shells on the rock salt beside each cup.

ALTERNATIVE SPECIES:
native oyster; Pacific oyster

Recipe by
Dietmar Sawyere

SERVES 6 AS AN ENTRÉE

1 tablespoon clarified butter (see page 89)

1 slice white sandwich bread, crusts discarded, cut into 5 mm dice

salt flakes, to taste

25 g unsalted butter

1 leek, white part only, washed well and thinly sliced

2½ tablespoons dry white wine

100 ml pouring cream

12 large Sydney rock oysters, freshly shucked (see page 121), on the half shell

vegetable oil, for deep-frying

40 g oscietra caviar

40 g salmon or ocean trout roe

2 teaspoons finely snipped chives

rock salt, for serving

rice flour, for dusting

Beignet batter

125 g plain flour

75 g rice flour

½ teaspoon baking powder

2 teaspoons honey

150 ml vodka

150 ml lager beer

Vichyssoise

25 g unsalted butter

150 g white onions, thinly sliced

350 g leeks, white part only, washed well and thinly sliced

700 ml Chicken stock (see Basics)

175 g floury potatoes, peeled and diced

25 ml oyster sauce (see Chefs' ingredients)

150 ml pouring cream

salt flakes, to taste

4 sheets titanium-grade leaf gelatine (see page 128)

Recipe by
Janni Kyritsis

OYSTERS ROCKEFELLER

SERVES 6 AS AN ENTRÉE

300 g salted butter

20 cm piece celery heart, chopped

8 spring onions (scallions), sliced

1 large handful flat-leaf parsley
leaves, chopped

2 tablespoons chopped French tarragon
(see Chefs' ingredients)

800 g baby spinach leaves,
stems discarded, finely chopped

3 tablespoons Pernod

¼ teaspoon Tabasco sauce,
more or less, to taste

salt flakes, to taste

2 cups (140 g) fine fresh breadcrumbs
(see Chefs' ingredients)

rock salt, for cooking and serving

36 Pacific oysters, freshly shucked
(see page 121), on the half shell

ALTERNATIVE SPECIES:
native oyster; Sydney rock oyster

This American classic was created in the late 1800s in Antoine's Restaurant in New Orleans and named after the oil magnate John D. Rockefeller because the sauce was so rich. While there are many bad versions of oysters Rockefeller, this version is lively with fresh green flavours and an aniseed tang from the tarragon and Pernod. Janni Kyritsis served it at MG Garage Restaurant in a dish called Oysters from Natural to Rockefeller, in which he presented a natural oyster alongside five others, each with a different topping. Oysters Rockefeller makes a particularly good introduction to oysters for those who aren't keen on eating them raw.

Heat the butter in a frying pan over low heat and cook the celery and spring onion until soft but not coloured. Add the parsley, tarragon and spinach and cook for 5–10 minutes, stirring occasionally, until the water has evaporated, leaving only the butter. Remove from the heat and stir in the Pernod, Tabasco sauce, salt and enough breadcrumbs to make a thick puree; you may not need them all. Transfer to a blender and process until very smooth; if there is too much liquid, add a few more breadcrumbs. The mixture should be thick enough that a wooden spoon will almost stand upright in it. Taste and add extra Tabasco sauce or salt if needed. Refrigerate until cold.

Preheat the oven to 260°C (fan-forced). Place the rock salt on a baking tray. Mound a generous spoonful of spinach mixture on top of each oyster in its shell and place on the baking tray. Refrigerate for 30 minutes, or until needed.

Place the oysters in the oven for 3–5 minutes, until the tops colour slightly, the spinach mixture is heated through and the oysters are just warmed but not cooked.

Serve the oysters on a bed of rock salt.

Recipe by
Frank Camorra

SCALLOPS BAKED IN THEIR SHELLS WITH WHITE WINE & BREADCRUMBS

SERVES 4 AS AN ENTRÉE

12 commercial scallops, on the half shell

2½ tablespoons extra virgin olive oil

1 white onion, finely diced

1 × 80 g piece jamón, diced

1 tablespoon Spanish unsmoked sweet paprika (see Chefs' ingredients)

500 ml albariño or other dry white wine

salt flakes, to taste

1 cup (70 g) coarse fresh breadcrumbs (see Chefs' ingredients)

ALTERNATIVE SPECIES:
blue mussel; surf clam

Frank Camorra's MoVida tapas bar in Melbourne's graffiti-splashed Hosier Lane redefined Spanish food in Australia. Named for the Madrid movement of youthful, patriotic free expression *La Movida Madrileña*, which swept Spain after Franco's death in 1975 (the same year the Camorra family moved to Australia), the restaurant is all about produce-driven shared dishes based on Spanish regional cooking. Jamón is Spanish raw ham; it's similar to Italian prosciutto, which you could substitute if it's not available. Spanish paprika is available from most delis and specialist provedores; it's worth buying it for an authentic Spanish flavour.

Preheat the oven to 180°C (fan-forced). Gently remove the scallops from their shells and trim off the small dark vein along the edge of the meat (see page 121), retaining the roe and any juices. Return the scallops to their shells.

Heat a frying pan over medium heat and add the oil. When hot, add the onion and cook for a minute. Stir in the jamón and cook for a further minute or so, until the onion just starts to colour. Stir in the paprika, cook for another minute, then stir in the wine. Bring to the boil, then reduce the heat and simmer until reduced by half. Remove from the heat.

Sprinkle the scallops with salt, spoon a tablespoon of the onion mixture over each one and sprinkle with breadcrumbs. Place in the oven for about 5 minutes, until the scallops are just cooked through and the breadcrumbs are lightly coloured.

ROAST DUCK, SCALLOP & EGGPLANT SALAD

Recipe by
Christine Manfield

In many cuisines, seafood is often combined with meat. This dish is from a class that Christine Manfield taught showcasing such combinations. Pick up a roast duck from a Chinese barbecue shop, then all you have to do is roast the eggplant and fry the scallops. If you don't have a gas stove, char the eggplant in a hot oven. It's important to buy 'dry' scallops that haven't been frozen or soaked in water; otherwise the water comes out as soon as they hit the pan, and they stew instead of frying.

For the eggplant salad, place the cumin seeds in a small frying pan (without any oil) and cook over medium heat, stirring frequently, until fragrant. Watch them closely as they can burn quickly. Grind the roasted cumin seeds to a powder using a mortar and pestle or spice grinder, then set aside.

Hold the eggplants with long-handled tongs and char over a flame until they are blackened and blistered all over. Peel, then squeeze out excess liquid from the flesh and chop finely. Heat a frying pan and add the oil. When hot, fry the onion and garlic until pale golden. Remove from the heat and combine with the cumin, eggplant and remaining salad ingredients and set aside.

Preheat the oven to 175°C (fan-forced).

Trim off the small dark vein along the edge of each scallop (see page 121). Brush the scallops with a little oil and sprinkle with salt and pepper. Set aside.

Whisk the vinegar, salt, pepper and remaining oil until emulsified. Set this dressing aside.

Remove the meat from the duck, discarding the carcass, and place on a baking tray in the oven for 5 minutes. Slice the meat into bite-sized pieces.

Meanwhile, heat a frying pan over high heat. When hot, cook the scallops for 1 minute, then turn and cook the other side for 30 seconds; remove them quickly from the pan to prevent overcooking.

Arrange the eggplant salad, duck, scallops, chopped coriander and mizuna in layers on plates, spooning the dressing between layers to season the duck and scallops. Finish with a garnish of coriander leaves on top and serve immediately.

SERVES 4 AS AN ENTRÉE

12 saucer scallops

100 ml extra virgin olive oil

salt flakes and freshly ground black pepper, to taste

1½ tablespoons sherry vinegar

1 Chinese roast duck

1 small handful coriander leaves, chopped, plus a few whole leaves to garnish

1 handful mizuna, stems removed

Eggplant salad

½ teaspoon cumin seeds

2 eggplants (aubergines)

3 tablespoons olive oil

2 tablespoons diced brown onion

5 cloves garlic, minced

1 small handful coriander leaves, chopped

1 teaspoon minced ginger

1 teaspoon salt flakes

½ teaspoon freshly ground black pepper

25 ml strained lemon juice

ALTERNATIVE SPECIES:
cuttlefish; loligo squid; southern calamari

Recipe by
David Thompson

HOT & SOUR SOUP
OF BLUE MUSSELS

SERVES 6 AS AN ENTRÉE

400 ml Chicken stock (see Basics)

2 stalks lemongrass, bruised

3 kaffir lime leaves, bruised

12 cherry tomatoes, lightly crushed

good pinch of deep-fried garlic

6 scud chillies, bruised

good pinch of salt

24 blue mussels, scrubbed and debearded (see page 121)

½ cup (125 ml) strained lime juice

4 tablespoons fish sauce (see Chefs' ingredients), more or less, to taste

1 large handful coriander leaves

ALTERNATIVE SPECIES:
pipi; prawn; surf clam; vongole

David Thompson coined the term 'scuds' to describe the fiercely hot tiny Thai chillies in the early 1990s, when scud missiles were being used in the Kuwait/Saudi conflict – implying that the use of these chillies can be almost as destructive. It's caught on and now many people refer to them by this name. They're available in Chinatown and Asian grocery stores, where they may be sold by their Thai name, *prik kii nuu suan* (literally 'mouse-dropping chillies'). This is a version of the classic Thai soup tom yum. As with all Thai recipes, the ingredients list is very flexible, so use it as a base and add different seafood or Asian mushrooms, such as oyster mushrooms or shimeji (in Thailand, fresh straw mushrooms are used). Traditionally, like all Thai dishes, this soup would be served alongside a number of other dishes as part of a meal, accompanied by steamed jasmine rice. To make deep-fried garlic, finely slice garlic and fry in hot oil for a minute or two, until golden, stirring with a spider to ensure it colours evenly, then drain on paper towel.

Place the stock, lemongrass, kaffir lime leaves, tomatoes, deep-fried garlic, 3 scuds and the salt in a saucepan and bring to the boil. Add the mussels, then reduce the heat, cover with a tight-fitting lid and simmer for a few minutes, until the mussels open.

Combine most of the lime juice, most of the fish sauce, the remaining scuds and coriander in a large serving bowl. Pour the simmering soup into the bowl. Taste and adjust the seasoning with the remaining lime juice and fish sauce if necessary; the soup should be salty, hot, sour and nutty from the deep-fried garlic. Ladle into soup bowls.

Recipe by
Damien Pignolet

HAZELNUT MUSSELS

SERVES 6 AS AN ENTRÉE

250 g shelled hazelnuts

2 kg blue mussels, scrubbed (see page 121)

1 clove garlic, crushed with a little salt

1½ cups (100 g) fine fresh breadcrumbs
(see Chefs' ingredients)

1 bunch chives, finely snipped

pinch of cayenne pepper

500 g unsalted butter, softened

4 tablespoons strained lemon juice

salt flakes, to taste

rock salt (optional) and lemon cheeks,
for serving

ALTERNATIVE SPECIES:
commercial scallop; oyster

This recipe was a huge hit when Damien Pignolet taught it at the Seafood School. Cooked this way, the mussels are simply irresistible – even people who weren't previously fond of mussels were converted! Damien credits Mogens Bay Esbensen, his business partner at Pavilion on the Park in the late 1970s, with showing him this way of preparing mussels. They're also great finger food; if you use the smallest mussels you can find, so much the better.

Preheat the oven to 160°C (fan-forced). Roast the hazelnuts on a baking tray for 5–10 minutes, until the skins split a little. Wrap the nuts in a tea towel and, while still very hot, rub well to remove most of the skin. Place the nuts in a food processor and pulse until they are just finely chopped; do not overwork them.

Pry the mussels open with a blunt knife, collecting the juices and discarding the empty half-shells. Separate the mussels from their shells, reserving the shells, and remove the beards.

Combine 2 tablespoons of the mussel juice with the garlic and 1 cup (70 g) of the breadcrumbs, then work in the chives, cayenne and butter to make a moist paste. Add the chopped hazelnuts and stir until smooth, adding more breadcrumbs if the paste doesn't hold together. Work in lemon juice to balance the taste and add a little salt and a little more cayenne if you like.

Place each mussel back in a half-shell and cover with the hazelnut butter, smoothing the top. Place them on a baking tray and refrigerate for at least 30 minutes, or until needed.

Preheat an overhead grill to the highest heat and grill the mussels for about 3 minutes, until lightly golden.

Arrange the mussels on a bed of rock salt, if using, and serve with lemon cheeks.

Recipe by
Giovanni Pilu

SPAGHETTI ALLE VONGOLE

SERVES 4 AS AN ENTRÉE

300 g spaghetti

½ cup (125 ml) extra virgin olive oil, plus extra for drizzling

600 g vongole, purged (see page 119)

2 cloves garlic, finely sliced

1 small red chilli, finely chopped

3 tablespoons dry white wine

1 handful flat-leaf parsley leaves, chopped

30 g bottarga, grated (optional)

ALTERNATIVE SPECIES:
blue mussel; surf clam

Giovanni Pilu likes to add a Sardinian twist to this classic vongole recipe with grated bottarga (air-dried mullet roe). Bottarga has a salty, fishy flavour; you can leave it out or add just a little if you prefer. The trick with such a simple dish lies in the quality of the ingredients, as there's nothing to disguise inferior produce. Use the best-quality olive oil you can afford and a good Italian wine that you'd be happy to drink (if it's not good enough to drink, it's not good enough to cook with!). Timing is also critical: the vongole must be opening just as the pasta is ready, so that neither is overcooked. The water clinging to the spaghetti when it's lifted into the frying pan combines with the oil, wine and liquid from the vongole to create a delicious sauce. It's important to toss the pasta thoroughly in the sauce, so that it emulsifies and becomes creamy; if it seems too dry, add another spoonful or two of the pasta cooking water and toss well to combine.

Bring a large saucepan of water to the boil and add salt. Add the spaghetti and cook until al dente.

Meanwhile, heat a large, deep frying pan over high heat and add the oil. When hot, add the vongole, garlic, chilli and wine. Cover with a tight-fitting lid, shake the pan well and cook for 3–4 minutes, shaking occasionally, until the shells open. Add half the parsley and half the bottarga (if using), and stir to combine well.

Using tongs, lift the cooked spaghetti from the water into the frying pan, and toss well to coat thoroughly and give the sauce a creamy consistency.

Serve scattered with the remaining parsley and bottarga (if using) and drizzled with olive oil.

WOK-TOSSED PIPIS WITH GARLIC, CHILLI & HOLY BASIL

Recipe by
Mark Jensen

It's a shame that pipis are often overlooked by cooks, as each smooth purple shell contains a delicious, bite-sized piece of meat; their unappreciated status means they can be a bargain, too. Like other clams that live in sandy areas, they need to be purged before cooking. If holy basil is unavailable, use Thai or purple basil. Woks come in a variety of shapes, sizes and materials, but Mark Jensen recommends a traditional thin carbon-steel wok (available cheaply in Chinatown). You'll need to season the wok before use. To do this, wash the wok well in warm soapy water and dry it thoroughly, then place over heat. Add 2 tablespoons of oil, wipe it all over the inside with paper towel and heat for 10–15 minutes. Wipe the wok out with paper towel and cool, then repeat the process. The wok is now ready to use. After using, wash the wok, place it over the heat for a few minutes to dry thoroughly, then wipe with a little oil to prevent rusting.

Bring about 3 litres of water to the boil in a wok or large saucepan and add a pinch of salt. Blanch the pipis, in small batches, for about 2 minutes, until the first one opens, then plunge them into iced water to refresh. Drain them in a colander. Take any pipis that are still firmly closed and, holding them away from the others, carefully open them using a blunt knife (such as a butter knife), and smell them to check that they are fresh, discarding any that aren't.

Heat a wok over medium heat and add the oil. Add the onion and garlic and cook for a minute or so, until soft but not coloured. Stir in the pipis, oyster sauce, chilli, half the basil and half the Vietnamese mint. Add the stock, salt, pepper and sugar, then cover and cook for a couple of minutes, shaking the wok occasionally, until the shells open wide.

Add the remaining mint and basil to the wok and stir in half the potato starch mixture. If the sauce doesn't thicken enough to coat the back of a wooden spoon, stir in more potato starch mixture, a little at a time, until the consistency is correct.

Serve the pipis with steamed jasmine rice.

SERVES 4

1 kg pipis, purged (see page 119)

1 tablespoon vegetable oil

1 small white onion, cut into eighths

2 teaspoons finely chopped garlic

1½ tablespoons oyster sauce (see Chefs' ingredients)

1 small red chilli, finely chopped

½ bunch holy basil, leaves picked

¼ bunch Vietnamese mint, leaves picked

1 cup (250 ml) Chicken stock (see Basics)

salt flakes and freshly ground white pepper, to taste

white sugar, to taste

2 tablespoons potato starch mixed with 2 tablespoons cold water

steamed jasmine rice, for serving

ALTERNATIVE SPECIES:
blue mussel; prawn; surf clam; vongole

Recipe by
Stefano Manfredi

ITALIAN FISH CHEEK & SHELLFISH SOUP

SERVES 6

1 × 1–1.5 kg red emperor head, fins on, scaled and gilled

1 large brown onion, roughly chopped

1 carrot, peeled and roughly chopped

1 celery heart, leaves attached, roughly chopped

6 cloves garlic, roughly chopped

1 cup (250 ml) extra virgin olive oil, plus extra for drizzling

1 cup (250 ml) tomato passata

a few sprigs thyme

salt flakes and freshly ground black pepper, to taste

18 slices sourdough baguette

18 blue mussels, scrubbed and debearded (see page 121)

18 vongole, purged (see page 119)

12 green (raw) prawns, peeled and deveined (see page 181)

1 small bunch flat-leaf parsley, leaves roughly chopped

ALTERNATIVE SPECIES:
head from bar rock cod or snapper

Popular all around the Mediterranean coast, hearty seafood soups make use of whatever fish and shellfish are readily, and usually cheaply, available. Nothing is wasted and fish heads, which contain plenty of meat, often end up in the soup pot. The bones add flavour and Stefano Manfredi says that the meat, especially from the cheeks, is a delicacy. Tomato passata is bottled Italian tomato sauce; if unavailable, use canned Italian tomatoes with their juice.

Wash the fish head well in cold water to remove any traces of blood. Place it in a saucepan and just cover with cold water. Bring to the boil, then reduce the heat and simmer for 20–30 minutes, until the cheek meat comes away from the bones easily. Strain, reserving the stock and the fish head. When the head is cool enough to handle, remove all the meat, shred it and set it aside, discarding the bones.

Place the onion, carrot, celery and 4 cloves of garlic in a food processor and mince finely. Heat a large saucepan over medium heat and add half the oil. When hot, add the minced mixture and cook for 6–8 minutes, until lightly coloured. Add the tomato passata, thyme and salt and bring to the boil, then reduce the heat and simmer for 15 minutes.

Meanwhile, finely mince the remaining 2 cloves of garlic and mix with the remaining oil. Brush the baguette slices with the oil mixture and place under an overhead grill for a few minutes on each side, until lightly browned.

Add enough of the reserved stock to the tomato sauce to achieve a thick soup consistency and bring to the boil. Add the mussels and vongole, then reduce the heat, cover with a tight-fitting lid and shake the pan well. Simmer for a minute or two, until the shells start to open. Add the prawns, fish-head meat and parsley and stir to combine well. Remove from the heat and stir in salt and pepper.

Divide the toasted baguette slices among shallow bowls and ladle the soup over the top. Serve drizzled with oil.

CEPHALOPODS

The name cephalopod comes from the Greek, meaning 'head-feet' — which pretty well sums up the appearance of squid, cuttlefish and octopuses! The most active of all molluscs, cephalopods generally don't have external shells, but they do have an ink sac from which they squirt a thick black ink to help distract predators. (The exception is a rarely seen sub-species of cephalopod, the nautilus, which has an external shell and doesn't have an ink sac).

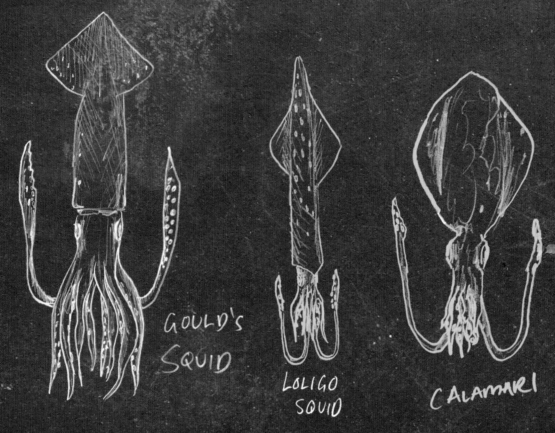

GOULD'S SQUID

LOLIGO SQUID

CALAMARI

SQUID

Squid are found worldwide; they range in size from tiny creatures measuring just 2.5 cm long to the infamous giant squid, the largest invertebrate on Earth, measuring up to 18 m long and weighing as much as 900 kg. They have a long, cylindrical head (also called a mantle, hood or tube), eight shorter arms and two longer tentacles and a thin, translucent, feather-shaped internal shell, known as a quill.

Calamari is the Italian word for squid, but the term also refers to those species of squid with side fins running the full length of their body, as opposed to those with relatively shorter side fins. Calamari are often more tender than other squid.

There are four main kinds of squid in Australia. Loligo squid, typically weighing about 100 g and 20 cm long, are the most common; they have mottled pinky-purple skin, long thin bodies and pointy side fins that run about half their length. Gould's squid are much larger (averaging 600–800 g) with smooth, light brownish-pink skin and hard suckers that must be sliced off their arms and tentacles. Southern calamari are a similar size to loligo squid and have mottled purpley-brown skin with long, rounded side fins running almost the full length of their body. The similar but larger northern calamari are found around Australia's northern coast.

CUTTLEFISH

Cuttlefish are very similar to squid, but have a broader, thicker head, shorter arms and a thick, calcified internal shell (the cuttlebone often seen in birds' cages). They are usually less expensive than squid and can be used interchangeably in almost any recipe. Cuttlefish ink is often used to make pasta, risotto and sauces black; it's sometimes referred to as 'squid ink', but it is the ink from cuttlefish that is used, as squid ink has a slightly bitter taste.

CUTTLEFISH

OCTOPUS

OCTOPUSES

Octopuses are found right around the Australian coast, from shallow tidal pools to ocean depths of more than 3000 m. They differ from squid and cuttlefish in that, while they all have eight arms, octopuses lack the two longer tentacles, side fins and internal shells. Their heads are also round instead of cylindrical. Octopuses need to be tenderised before being cooked; traditionally fishermen beat them against the rocks to do this, but today they're usually tumbled in a small cement mixer.

CHOOSING, STORING & COOKING CEPHALOPODS

Cephalopods are relatively inexpensive and good value as there's very little waste. They're also very easy to clean and prepare, so it's worthwhile buying whole fresh Australian products rather than frozen, already cleaned, imported ones.

When choosing cephalopods, look for:

* brightly coloured, lustrous skin;
* firm and intact flesh and tentacles;
* no discolouration;
* a pleasant fresh sea smell.

Buy whole squid and clean them yourself, rather than buying pre-cleaned squid tubes that are often imported frozen.

To store squid, cuttlefish and octopuses, clean and rinse them, then place on a plate or tray or in a lidded container. Cover with a damp cloth and then with plastic wrap or the lid. Store in the coldest part of the fridge and use within 2–3 days.

All cephalopods must be cooked either briefly over high heat or for a long time over low heat. Anything in between and they become tough and chewy. Before cooking squid and cuttlefish, it's also important to wipe both sides of the hood firmly with paper towel to remove the membrane that otherwise makes them chewy. Although their skin is usually peeled off, squid, cuttlefish and octopus can be cooked with the skin on if you wish; it turns a dark purple when cooked.

PREPARING SQUID

1

Grasp the arms and tentacles. Pull firmly to separate the head from the tube (try not to break the ink sac as the ink stains).

2

Cut below the eyes. Discard the eyes and everything above them.

3

Push the beak (mouth) out from between the arms. The tentacles and arms can also be washed and used.

4

Remove the quill from inside the tube.

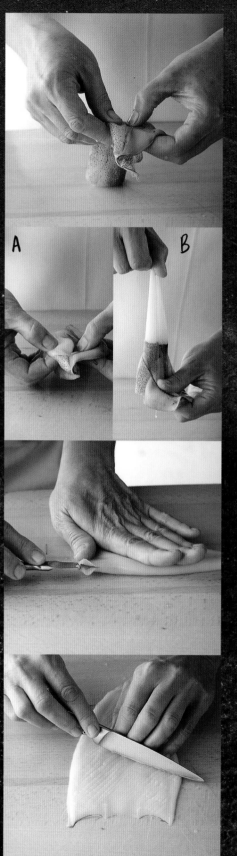

5

Push your thumb between the tube and a side fin to break the skin.

6

(A) Holding the side fins, twist the tip of the tube to pull it away from the skin. (B) Grasp the side fins and pull down to peel off the skin around the tube; the side fins can also be peeled and used.

7

If you are cutting the tube into rings, wash the inside well to remove any remaining gut; otherwise, place the knife inside the tube and cut it open along the obvious seam. Lay the tube out flat and, working across the tube (not from top to bottom), wipe both sides firmly with paper towel to remove any remaining intestines and membrane.

8

To honeycomb the squid, hold the knife at a 30-degree angle and score the inside of the tube on the diagonal. Turn the tube around 180 degrees and score again to create a crosshatch pattern. If slicing tubes that haven't been honeycombed, cut from the top to the bottom of the tube to prevent curling.

PREPARING CUTTLEFISH

1

Grasp the cuttlebone, through the tube, between thumb and forefinger and twist. The cuttlebone will cut through the skin and come away easily; discard the bone.

2

Using your thumb to split the firm flesh away from the membrane, tear the tube open along the line where the cuttlebone was, starting from the base.

3

Working from one side, break the intestinal sac (with arms and tentacles attached) away from the tube.

4

Cut below the eyes; discard eyes and everything above them. Rinse, especially if the ink sac is broken. The arms and tentacles can also be washed and used.

5

Push the beak (mouth) out from between the arms.

6

Place the tube on a chopping board, skin-side down. Grasp a small side fin on one side and, using your thumb to separate the skin from the flesh, peel the flesh away from skin.

7

Lay out flat and, working across the tube (not from top to bottom), wipe both sides firmly with paper towel to remove any remaining membrane. To honeycomb, see Step 8 opposite. If slicing tubes that haven't been honeycombed, cut from the top to the bottom of the tube to prevent curling.

PREPARING OCTOPUS

1 Holding the head, slice between the arms and eyes.

2 Cut off the head, just above the eyes, and set aside. Discard the eyes.

3 Push the beak (mouth) out from between the arms.

4 Place the knife just inside the white side of the head, being careful not to pierce the ink sac; cut the head open.

5 Use your thumbs to peel back the head to expose the intestinal sac.

6 Working from one side, break the intestinal sac away from the inside of the head (try not to break the ink sac); discard. Place the head on a chopping board, skin side down. Grasp the skin on one side and, using your thumb to separate the skin from flesh, peel the flesh away from the skin.

7 Rinse the head or wipe with a clean, damp cloth. Cut the head and arms into pieces for cooking.

Recipe by
Peter Gilmore

SEARED BABY SQUID WITH RADISHES, NASTURTIUMS & AÏOLI

SERVES 6 AS AN ENTRÉE

12 baby red radishes, trimmed and halved

24 baby French breakfast radishes, trimmed

2 cured chorizo, peeled, halved and cut into 5 mm-thick slices

75 ml extra virgin olive oil

1 kg small loligo squid, cleaned but not skinned, tentacles reserved (see page 154)

salt flakes, to taste

Aïoli (see Basics), for serving

24 nasturtium leaves

24 radish flowers

6 nasturtium flowers, petals separated

ALTERNATIVE SPECIES:
cuttlefish; saucer scallop

Peter Gilmore's dishes are often colourful with tiny edible flowers and unusual leaves. Nasturtiums grow like weeds in most gardens and their leaves have a lovely peppery flavour, so it's worth planting some to colour and spice up your salads. Many greengrocers also sell edible flowers; use whatever is available. French breakfast radishes are elongated red and white radishes. For this recipe, the smaller the squid the better. If only large squid are available, slice the tubes into bite sized pieces before cooking.

Boil the radishes in salted water for 1 minute, then refresh in iced water. Drain and set aside.

Heat a non-stick frying pan and fry the chorizo until lightly coloured. Remove from the pan and set aside, covered to keep warm. Wipe out the frying pan and reheat. Drizzle 2½ tablespoons of the oil over the squid and sprinkle generously with salt. Sear the squid, including the tentacles, in batches, for 20 seconds on each side. Remove from the pan and set aside, covered to keep warm.

Spread some aïoli onto each plate, and arrange the squid and chorizo around the plate.

Toss the radishes and nasturtium leaves with the remaining oil and sprinkle with salt. Scatter over the plates and garnish with the radish flowers and nasturtium petals. Add a couple of dots of aioli. Serve immediately.

Recipe by
Tim Pak Poy

CRISP RICE CAKES WITH SQUID BRAISED IN OLIVE OIL & TOMATO

SERVES 6

750 g small loligo squid, cleaned and tentacles reserved (see page 154)

1 tablespoon yellow rock sugar, pounded

3 tablespoons extra virgin olive oil

24 kalamata olives

6 dried long red chillies, soaked in warm water for 10 minutes, then drained

9 slices peeled ginger

2 stems curry leaves

2 cloves garlic, minced

400 g tinned whole peeled tomatoes, crushed in the hand

juice of ½ lemon

2 tablespoons black sesame seeds

400 g short-grain rice

1 spring onion (scallion), minced

1 egg, lightly beaten

2 cups (200 g) panko breadcrumbs

olive oil, for shallow-frying

salt flakes, to taste

coriander leaves, for garnishing

ALTERNATIVE SPECIES:
cuttlefish; octopus; southern calamari

Tim Pak Poy cooked brilliantly complex dishes at Claude's for over 15 years, but at home he's always preferred rustic recipes such as this one. The dish works best with tiny squid, ideally the size of your little finger. If they aren't available, use the smallest squid you can find, slice them in half crossways, push the tentacles into the top half and slice the bottom half into strips. This tastes just as good at room temperature as it does hot; you could serve it with a salad of sliced cherry tomatoes, cucumber and witlof, if you like. Yellow rock sugar is available from Asian grocery stores, but white sugar could be substituted. Panko are Japanese breadcrumbs; just use regular breadcrumbs if they're unavailable.

Push the tentacles into the squid tubes and pat dry. Toss the squid in the rock sugar and lay them on paper towel.

Heat a deep heavy-based frying pan over medium heat and add the extra virgin olive oil. When hot, add the olives, chillies and 6 slices of ginger and cook for a couple of minutes, until the sizzling subsides – but be careful not to burn the chillies. Add the curry leaves and stir for a few seconds, then, using a slotted spoon, remove the olives, chillies, ginger and curry leaves from the oil and set aside.

Increase the heat and when the oil is just starting to smoke, add the squid and garlic and toss well to coat. Add the tomatoes, squeeze in the lemon juice then add the lemon half to the pan. Add the reserved olives, chillies, ginger and curry leaves.

Reduce the heat to low, cover and cook until the squid is tender, about 50 minutes. Remove the lid and continue cooking for 5–10 minutes, until the liquid has reduced to a sauce consistency.

Meanwhile, place the sesame seeds in a small frying pan (without any oil) and cook over medium heat, stirring frequently, until lightly coloured and aromatic; watch them closely as they can burn quickly. Steam the rice in a rice cooker or according to the packet instructions, then, using a fork, lightly fluff up the rice. Mince the remaining ginger and mix through the rice with the spring onion and sesame seeds.

Lay a piece of plastic wrap in the palm of one hand and place about 1½ tablespoons of rice mixture in the centre. Gather the plastic wrap around it, twisting the top to form a neat ball. Unwrap and set the rice ball aside; repeat with the remaining mixture. Dip the rice balls in egg, then roll them in the panko breadcrumbs, patting them to coat well.

Heat the olive oil in a wok or frying pan and shallow-fry the rice cakes for a few minutes on each side, until crisp and golden. Drain on paper towel and sprinkle with salt.

Gently break open the rice balls and place them in bowls. Spoon some squid and sauce into the centre of each ball and scatter with coriander leaves.

SALAD OF SOUTHERN CALAMARI, EGGPLANT, TOMATO & MINT

Recipe by
Jonathan Barthelmess

Calamari are often more tender than other squid, and shaving them finely makes them even more so. This dish, which was often on the menu when Jonathan Barthelmess was at Coast restaurant at Darling Harbour, is a delicious way to eat calamari or squid. As the calamari is only very briefly warmed in the oil, it's essential that you buy sashimi-grade, the freshest possible.

Place the tomatoes with their juices, lemon juice, chilli, half the mint, salt, pepper, half the garlic and 2 tablespoons of the oil in a bowl. Cover with plastic wrap and set aside for 1 hour at room temperature.

Meanwhile, heat a frying pan over medium heat and add 1 cup (250 ml) of the oil. When hot, add the eggplant, salt and pepper and cook for a few minutes, until soft but not coloured. Stir the remaining garlic through the eggplant, then remove the eggplant from the oil and place on paper towel. Sprinkle with salt and pepper and leave to cool.

Cut the calamari tube in half lengthways and, using a sharp knife, shave it as finely as possible. Heat half the remaining oil in a small saucepan over low heat. Add half the calamari and cook for about 15 seconds, until it just turns white; it should be just warmed through, not coloured. Remove it from the pan, place on paper towel and sprinkle with salt and pepper. Repeat with the remaining oil and calamari.

Divide the eggplant among plates and top with the calamari. Drizzle with the tomato mixture, sprinkle with pepper and remaining mint and serve at room temperature.

SERVES 6

1 kg vine-ripened tomatoes, peeled, seeded and cut into 1 cm dice, juices reserved

juice of 1 lemon, strained

2 small green chillies, seeded and finely chopped

1 large handful mint leaves, very finely sliced

salt flakes and freshly ground white pepper, to taste

4 cloves garlic, minced

2 cups (500 ml) extra virgin olive oil

4 eggplants (aubergines), peeled and diced

1.5 kg sashimi-grade southern calamari, cleaned (see page 154), tentacles and flaps discarded

ALTERNATIVE SPECIES:
cuttlefish; loligo squid

Recipe by
Lucio Galletto

CUTTLEFISH & PEAS

SERVES 6 AS AN ENTRÉE

1 kg cuttlefish, cleaned and tentacles reserved (see page 155)

3 tablespoons extra virgin olive oil

1 clove garlic, finely chopped

1 small white onion, finely chopped

½ small carrot, finely chopped

1 tablespoon chopped flat-leaf parsley

1 stem marjoram, leaves picked

1 stem oregano, leaves picked

salt flakes and freshly ground black pepper, to taste

4 tablespoons dry white wine

1.4 kg green peas, shelled (to yield about 500 g shelled peas)

ALTERNATIVE SPECIES:
loligo squid; southern calamari

Lucio Galletto is not a chef: he is always very quick to make this clear. He is, however, a restaurateur of some note, having run the floor of his eponymous Sydney restaurant for over 30 years and, although he's too shy to say so, he's also a very good cook, especially when he turns his hand to simple home-style Italian classics, such as this dish, called *seppie e piselli* in Italian. *Seppie*, the Italian for cuttlefish, is the origin of the English word sepia, as cuttlefish ink was once used as a writing ink which had the distinctive brown tones of what later became known as sepia photographs.

Slice the cuttlefish tubes into 1 cm-wide strips and leave the tentacles intact. Heat a flameproof terracotta pot or high-sided frying pan over low heat and add the oil. When hot, add the garlic, onion, carrot, parsley, marjoram and oregano and cook for 3 minutes, stirring with a wooden spoon. Increase the heat to medium, add the cuttlefish, salt and pepper and cook for 8 minutes or so, stirring regularly, until nicely coloured.

Add the wine and cook for a minute or two, until it evaporates, then add the peas. Mix well, add 1½ tablespoons of water, then cover and reduce the heat to very low. Cook for about 15 minutes, stirring from time to time, until tender; if it starts to dry out before the peas are cooked, add a little more water. Serve hot.

Recipe by
Lauren Murdoch

CHILLI SALT OCTOPUS WITH ALMOND SKORDALIA

3 × 500 g octopus, cleaned (see page 157)

rind of 1 lemon

4 cloves garlic, peeled

4 stalks parsley

vegetable oil, for deep-frying

Almond skordalia

50 g blanched almonds

4 cloves garlic, roughly chopped

1 egg yolk

1 tablespoon strained lemon juice

½ teaspoon fine sea salt

½ teaspoon freshly ground white pepper

½ cup (125 ml) olive oil

4 tablespoons fine fresh breadcrumbs
(see Chefs' ingredients)

Beer batter

1 cup (150 g) plain flour

1 tablespoon fine sea salt

1 tablespoon chilli powder

1½ cups (375 ml) beer

ALTERNATIVE SPECIES:
cuttlefish or squid (no need to cook in oven, just dust in flour and deep-fry)

Lauren Murdoch taught this recipe at the Seafood School in a class entitled 'Bites for Drinks', and it is a very moreish nibble to serve with pre-dinner drinks or as finger food. The beer batter is light, salty and spicy; you can add more beer, flour, salt or chilli to suit your taste if you like. The octopus braises in its own juices in the oven – the cooking time can vary quite a bit depending on how well it's been tenderised when you buy it. Once braised and cooled, it can be sliced and served as a salad with garlic, spring onion, plenty of flat-leaf parsley and a vinaigrette dressing. Lauren was sous chef to Janni Kyritsis at MG Garage restaurant for five years, and this is his skordalia recipe. In Greece, it is the traditional accompaniment to fried fish or vegetables, but you could also serve the octopus with just a squeeze of lemon.

To make the skordalia, place the almonds and garlic in a food processor and pulse into fine crumbs. Add the egg yolk, lemon juice, salt and pepper and blend to combine. With the motor running, slowly pour in the oil. Add the breadcrumbs and mix until well combined. Add enough water (about 100 ml) to achieve the consistency of thickened cream. Refrigerate until needed. Skordalia thickens as it sits, so add a little extra water if needed to achieve the desired consistency before serving. This makes about 300 ml.

To make the beer batter, sift the flour into a bowl. Place the salt and chilli powder in a frying pan and cook over high heat for a minute or so, until very hot but not burnt. Add to the flour and mix to combine. Pour in the beer, then mix gently into a batter; it should still be a little lumpy.

Preheat the oven to 175°C (fan-forced). Place the octopus in a glass or ceramic lidded baking dish just large enough to hold them in a single layer, then add the lemon rind, garlic and parsley. Press a sheet of baking paper onto the surface of the octopus and cover tightly with a double layer of foil, then the lid. Cook for 1–2 hours until a wooden skewer can easily pierce the thickest part of the tentacles. Remove from the oven, open the foil and set aside to cool a little, then refrigerate the octopus in its own liquid until cold. Separate the tentacles from the heads and slice the bodies into large strips.

Preheat the vegetable oil to 180°C (see page 61). Dip the octopus pieces into the batter, allowing any excess to drain off, then carefully lower them into the oil, in batches, and deep-fry until golden.

Serve immediately with almond skordalia on the side for dipping.

Recipe by
Frank Camorra

GALICIAN-STYLE OCTOPUS

SERVES 6 AS AN ENTRÉE

3 red capsicums (peppers)

1 head of garlic

2 tablespoons extra virgin olive oil,
plus extra for drizzling

salt flakes, to taste

Spanish unsmoked sweet paprika
(see Chefs' ingredients), to taste

3 × 350 g octopus tentacles,
rinsed under cold water

1 kg kipfler potatoes, peeled

ALTERNATIVE SPECIES:
Gould's squid

Galicia is the north-western region of Spain. With the Atlantic Ocean to its west and the Bay of Biscay to its north, it's no surprise that seafood features strongly in its cuisine. While small octopuses are easily cooked by throwing them in a hot pan or on the barbecue, it can be a bit more daunting tackling larger specimens. Frank Camorra's technique of plunging the tentacles into water several times before simmering them helps to set the gelatinous coating on the outside of the tentacles – which is the most highly prized part of the octopus in Spain.

Preheat the oven to 180°C (fan-forced). Place the capsicums and garlic on a baking tray, drizzle them with oil and sprinkle with a pinch of salt. Cook for 20 minutes, then remove the garlic and set aside. Continue cooking the capsicums for a further 15 minutes or so, until the skin blackens. Reserve the cooking juices and set the capsicums aside until cool enough to handle, then peel them, discarding the seeds, skin and stalks. Place the capsicum flesh in a blender, squeeze in the pulpy flesh of the garlic and add the paprika, salt flakes and capsicum cooking juices. Blend until smooth, then cover and set aside.

Bring a large saucepan of water to a rapid boil. Using a pair of tongs, plunge the tentacles into the water for 15 seconds, then remove. Wait for the water to return to the boil, then repeat the plunging three more times, holding the tentacles in the water for 15 seconds each time and waiting for the water to return to the boil before doing it again.

Place the tentacles in the water one last time and leave them there, then add the potatoes and reduce the heat to a bare simmer. Cook for 30–40 minutes, until the tentacles and potatoes are tender; the outside layer of the tentacles should be pink but intact and a knife should pierce the flesh without too much resistance. Gently lift the tentacles and potatoes out of the saucepan and set aside until cool enough to handle. Discard the cooking liquid.

Slice the tentacles and potatoes into 1.5 cm-thick discs. Spoon the capsicum puree onto a platter and arrange the octopus and potatoes on top in a random fashion. Sprinkle with a little extra paprika and salt flakes, drizzle with oil and serve.

ITALIAN SEAFOOD SALAD WITH PESTO, POTATOES & GREEN BEANS

Insalata di mare (seafood salad) is a very popular antipasto in Italy. This one, which reminds Lucio Galletto of his childhood in a restaurant family on the Ligurian coast, is vibrant with the region's best-known condiment, pesto. Meaning 'pound' in Italian, pesto was traditionally made by pounding small basil leaves with pine nuts, cheese and Liguria's mild olive oil; the resulting paste, which could be stored for months, added a splash of summer to soups, pastas and salads during the long winter months when fresh herbs weren't available. Lucio likes the harmony and balance of this combination of seafood, but if some are unavailable you can still make the salad. The pesto here is made without cheese and with a little anchovy added, as this flavour marries better with the seafood. The recipe makes more than you'll need for this dish, but leftover pesto can be stored in the fridge for a few weeks covered with a thin layer of oil, and served drizzled over any grilled seafood or meat, or tossed through pasta. Potatoes and green beans are traditional ingredients of Liguria's *pasta al pesto*, giving them a particular synergy in this delicious warm salad.

To make the pesto, place the anchovy, garlic and a little salt in a mortar and grind with a pestle to form a coarse paste, working the pestle in a rotary motion. Add the basil and pound to incorporate. Add the pine nuts and continue grinding until a coarse paste forms. Transfer to a bowl, and slowly add the oil, mixing with a wooden spoon to emulsify. Set aside.

Slice the cuttlefish and squid tubes into 1 cm-wide strips and halve the tentacles. Cut the octopuses into individual tentacles and slice the heads into strips. Bring a saucepan of water to the boil and add the cuttlefish, squid and octopus. Return to the boil, then reduce the heat and simmer for 3–5 minutes, until opaque. Remove using a slotted spoon and place in a bowl.

Return the water to the boil and add prawns and scampi; return to the boil, then reduce the heat and simmer for 1–2 minutes, until the flesh is just opaque. Drain and set aside. Peel the scampi and add them and the prawns to the bowl.

Boil the potatoes in salted water for 3 minutes, then remove using a slotted spoon and set aside. Return the water to the boil, then add the beans and boil for 2 minutes. Drain.

Add the beans to the bowl of seafood and toss gently with lemon juice, oil, salt and pepper.

Rub the surface of six plates with the cut surface of the garlic, then discard it. Arrange the potato slices in the centre and top with seafood and beans. Drizzle with a little of the juices from the bowl and the pesto, to taste. Sprinkle with pine nuts and serve.

Recipe by
Lucio Galletto

SERVES 6

3 small cuttlefish, cleaned and tentacles reserved (see page 155)

3 loligo squid, cleaned and tentacles reserved (see page 154)

4 × 75–100 g baby octopus, cleaned (see page 157)

400 g green (raw) prawns, peeled, deveined and tails intact (see page 181)

6 scampi, halved and deveined (see page 181)

2 large waxy potatoes, peeled and thinly sliced

100 g green beans, topped, tailed and cut into fine matchsticks

juice of 1 lemon, strained

3 tablespoons extra virgin olive oil

salt flakes and freshly ground black pepper, to taste

1 clove garlic, peeled and halved

1 tablespoon pine nuts, chopped

Pesto

1 anchovy fillet in oil (see Chefs' Ingredients), drained

1 large clove garlic, peeled

salt flakes, to taste

2 bunches basil, small leaves only, picked

1 tablespoon pine nuts

75 ml extra virgin olive oil

ALTERNATIVE SPECIES:
southern calamari

CRUSTACEANS

Crustaceans are a very large group, consisting of over 50,000 species, including some of the most familiar — and popular — shellfish, such as prawns, crabs, rocklobsters and bugs. All of these edible crustaceans belong to the order 'decapod' (meaning ten-footed). They all have a shell that they shed and replace as they grow. Despite being various colours in their raw state, all crustaceans turn red when cooked because their shells contain a carotenoid pigment called astaxanthin (the best known carotenoid pigment is carotene, which gives carrots their bright orange colour). Astaxanthin's colour isn't obvious in live or raw shellfish because it's bound with a protein that usually creates a blue-green colour: astaxanthin is heat-stable and the protein isn't, so when heat is applied the protein is destroyed, releasing the pigment and giving the typical red colour of cooked shellfish.

BLUE SWIMMER CRAB

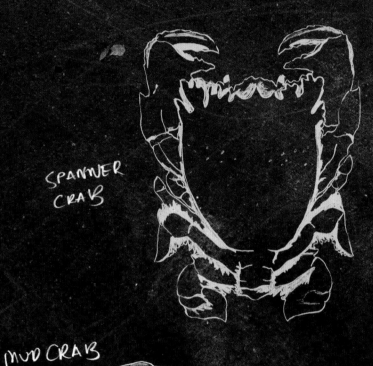

SPANNER CRAB

MUD CRAB

CRABS

Australia has three main species of edible crabs. *Blue swimmer crabs*, with their distinctive mottled bright blue to purple-brown shell, typically weigh around 200–300 g. They are one of the few crustaceans not sold live, as they don't survive well once caught. *Mud crabs*, found mainly on the muddy bottoms of shallow coastal mangroves, have large front legs and developed claws and generally weigh 500 g–1 kg. *Spanner crabs* have spanner-shaped front claws and long, almost goblet-shaped, bright orange shells (even when live). They weigh about 400 g and are usually sold cooked, although they can occasionally be found live. Spanner crabs have a lower yield than other crabs and so are also lower priced.

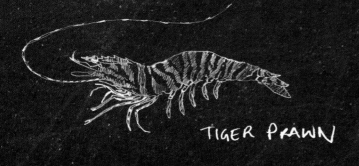

TIGER PRAWN

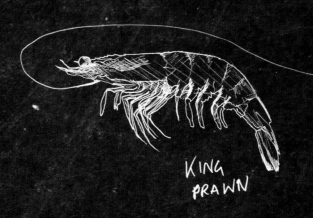

KING PRAWN

SCHOOL PRAWN

SCAMPI

PRAWNS

Prawns are one of the most versatile and widely available seafoods worldwide. There are several different prawn species commonly sold in Australia. *Tiger prawns*, the most common aquaculture prawn, have distinct grey, blue or black stripes. *King prawns* have a cream to light brown body and distinctive blue tailfin. They are generally sold larger than tiger prawns (though the name 'king' does not refer to their size); the legs are bright blue in western king prawns and cream in eastern king prawns. *Redspot prawns* are a type of king prawn, though often smaller, with a distinctive red spot on each side of their body shell. *Banana prawns*, caught off northern Australia, are translucent to yellow with tiny dark spots; they are also farmed. *School prawns* and *bay prawns* have translucent brown to green bodies with dark brown speckling and green tips on the tail fan; they're often sold small enough to eat shell and all. There is often confusion between the words prawn and shrimp. In the United States, shrimp is the common term, even for large specimens, while in Britain, shrimp is used for smaller specimens and prawn refers to the larger ones. In Australia, prawn is used for all sizes.

SCAMPI

Scampi look like a cross between a prawn and a lobster. They have curved prawn-like bodies and long developed front nippers. The word scampi comes from the Italian name for these creatures; in other parts of the world, they are variously called Norway lobsters, Dublin Bay prawns and langoustines. They are caught off the Western Australia coast and in New Zealand waters, and are generally snap-frozen at sea as they deteriorate very quickly once caught.

EASTERN
ROCKLOBSTER

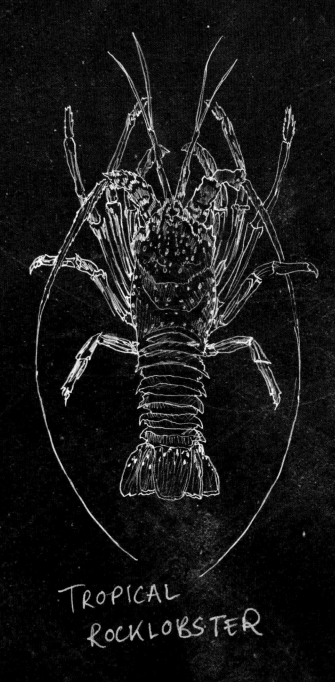

TROPICAL
ROCKLOBSTER

ROCKLOBSTERS

Known as spiny lobsters in most parts of the world, rocklobsters are higher priced than most
crustaceans. They shouldn't be confused with the 'true' lobsters of the northern hemisphere,
the main differences being that 'true' lobsters have huge claws or nippers, containing a significant
proportion of meat, and much smaller antennae. There are four rocklobster species in Australia.
Eastern rocklobsters, the world's largest rocklobsters (recorded up to 8 kg), are found around Australia's
south-eastern coast; they have a green-black shell and smooth tail. *Southern rocklobsters* are found
around the southern coast, including around Tasmania; they look similar to eastern, with their short
antennae, but their shell is rough-textured and orange-red. *Western rocklobsters*, native to Australia
and found along Western Australia's mid- to south coast, are the most valuable commercial marine
species in Australia and most are exported live or frozen to Japan, Taiwan or China; they have
a reddish-purple shell and very long antennae. *Tropical rocklobsters* are mainly caught in the Torres Strait,
by spear or hand; they are often intricately patterned (especially the legs), with very long antennae.

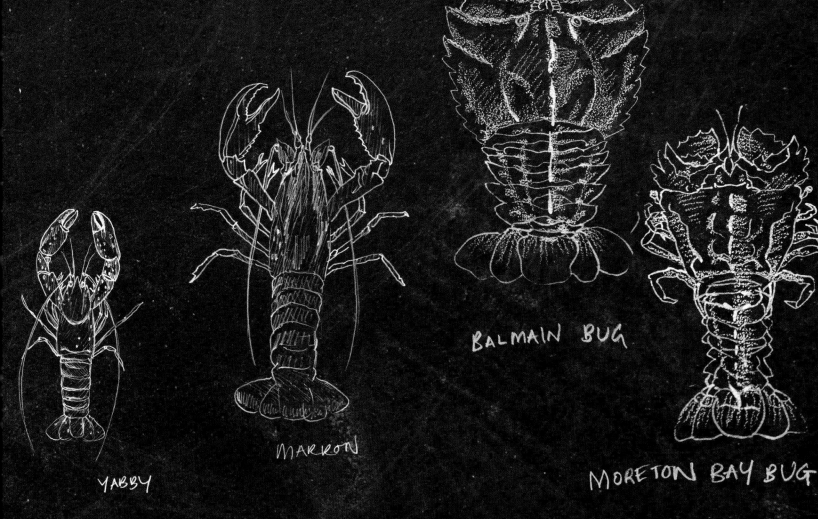

BALMAIN BUG

MARRON

YABBY

MORETON BAY BUG

FRESHWATER CRAYFISH

Freshwater crayfish (called crawfish in the USA) look rather like miniature northern hemisphere lobsters with large front nippers. They're found in waterholes, dams, swamps, creeks and billabongs all over Australia, though the ones available commercially are now almost exclusively farmed. There are three main types of freshwater crayfish. *Yabbies*, which are found throughout south-eastern Australia and south-western Queensland, are the most common. The very similar *redclaws* are native to tropical Queensland and the Northern Territory, and named for the distinctive red patches on the outside of the males' front claws. *Marrons*, the largest and most highly prized freshwater crayfish, are indigenous to south-western Western Australia, and have also been introduced to Kangaroo Island in South Australia.

BUGS

Closely related to rocklobsters, bugs are one of Australia's most sought-after seafood species. In other parts of the world, they are known as shovel-nosed, bay, squat or slipper lobsters. There are two main types of bugs available in Australia: *Balmain bugs*, which are found all around the southern half of Australia, and *Moreton Bay bugs*, which, despite their name, are found much further afield than Queensland's Moreton Bay, living around the northern half of Australia's coast. The two types are almost identical, but can easily be told apart by the position of the eyes: Moreton Bay bugs' are on the outer edges of their shells, while Balmain bugs' are close to the centre of their heads.

CHOOSING, STORING & COOKING CRUSTACEANS

Crustaceans, with the exception of prawns, scampi and blue swimmer crabs, are usually sold live. It's best to avoid crustaceans sold raw and dead, as it's hard to tell how fresh they are, and the flesh deteriorates very quickly. Raw crustaceans are called 'green' – meaning 'uncooked' rather than as a reference to their colour. They actually vary in colour from species to species when raw, although all turn red when cooked.

Most live crabs, freshwater crayfish and, sometimes, rocklobsters are stored out of the water. If possible, buy bugs and rocklobsters live from a tank.

When choosing live crustaceans, look for:

* signs of liveliness;
* a hard shell – this indicates that they haven't recently moulted;
* intact limbs and antennae.

When choosing dead crustaceans, look for:

* brightly coloured, lustrous shells;
* firm, intact heads and shells;
* no discolouration, especially at the joints;
* a pleasant fresh sea smell.

Whether bought live or dead, crustaceans should be consumed as soon as possible after purchase.

Store live crustaceans in a covered container, with ventilation holes in the top and wet butcher's paper or cloth in the bottom. Keep them in the coolest part of the house (below 20°C) for up to 2 days. Live bugs won't survive long out of the water and deteriorate quickly once dead, so cook them on the day they're purchased.

Store dead crustaceans in the coolest part of the fridge, in a lidded container or on a plate or tray covered with plastic wrap for 2–3 days.

It's always preferable to buy seafood just before you intend to eat it. However, if you want to freeze prawns, you can place them, unpeeled, in a lidded plastic container appropriate to the volume of prawns. Cover with water (do not add salt, as it will draw out moisture from the prawns), then seal, date and freeze for up to 3 months at -18°C (many domestic freezers do not get this low; if in doubt, check). This forms a large iceblock, which insulates the prawns. Frozen Australian crabmeat is a great product to keep in the freezer for a quick meal. Press it gently in a sieve before using to remove excess moisture and check it for any small fragments of cartilage or shell. Always thaw frozen seafood in the fridge, never at room temperature.

The easiest and most humane way to kill any live crustacean is to first chill it in the freezer for 30–60 minutes (depending on size) until it becomes insensible, but not long enough to freeze it solid, then place it into a large saucepan of rapidly boiling water and put the lid on to return the water to the boil as quickly as possible. It is neither humane nor good cooking practice to put a crustacean that hasn't first been well chilled into boiling water, as the stress will render the meat tough. The RSPCA website (rspca.org.au) provides further details.

The crustacean can then be removed and prepared according to the recipe, or boiled until cooked. Cook in rapidly boiling salted water (½ cup or 150 g table salt to 2.5 litres water), timing from when the crustaceans are put into the boiling water. When cooked, set aside to cool; do not refresh in iced water.

Using this method, cook:

* mud crabs and rocklobsters for 1 minute per 100 g;
* blue swimmer crabs, marrons and bugs for 1 minute per 50 g;
* prawns, yabbies, redclaw and scampi for 1 minute per 25 g average body weight.

PREPARING CRABS

Live crabs should be humanely killed before you prepare them as below; see page 179 for details.

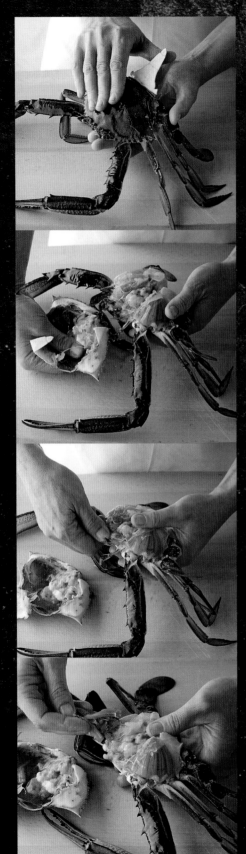

1

Lift up the flap attached to the back of the top shell. Insert thumb under flap and use to lever the top shell off towards the front.

2

Most of the inedible organs will come away with the shell.

3

Break off the eyes and the shell holding them in place.

4

Lift out and discard the grey feathery gills ('dead man's fingers') from the body.

5

Use a small spoon to remove the remaining internal organs. Wipe with a clean, damp cloth.

6

Twist off the large front legs.

7

(A) Quarter the body. (B) Crack the large legs and nippers with crab crackers (see Seafood kit) so the flavours and heat can penetrate.

8

If using meat from cooked crabs, use a crab pick (see Seafood kit) to extract it from the body and legs, checking carefully for bits of cartilage.

PREPARING GREEN (RAW) PRAWNS

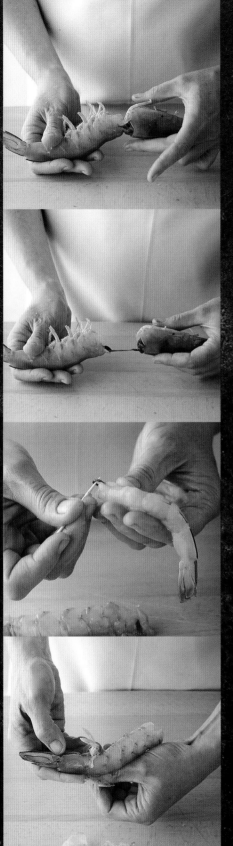

1

Holding the prawn on its back and breaking from the underside, gently break the head away from the body.

2

Hold the prawn straight and gently pull the head away from the body; the digestive tract will usually come out in one go, attached to the head.

3

If the digestive tract breaks off, grasp it and, holding the prawn straight, gently pull it out or use a thin wooden skewer or toothpick to hook it out from the back of the prawn. Alternatively, make a small incision along the back of the prawn to remove the tract.

4

Break off the legs until you reach the tail, then peel off the shell; if keeping the tail fin on, leave the last section of shell on to hold fin in place.

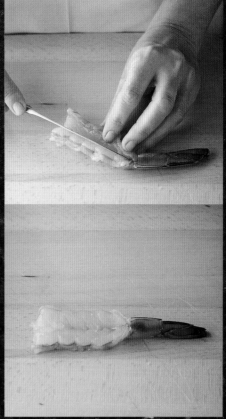

5

To butterfly a prawn, lay it on its side and slice two-thirds of the way along the back of the prawn. Wipe away any digestive tract.

6

Lay the prawn on a chopping board, cut-side down, and press gently with the heel of your hand to flatten it out.

SCAMPI CAN BE PREPARED IN THE SAME WAY AS PRAWNS OR SPLIT AND PREPARED IN THE SAME WAY AS BUGS.

PREPARING ROCKLOBSTERS

Live rocklobsters should be humanely killed before you prepare them as below; see page 179 for details.

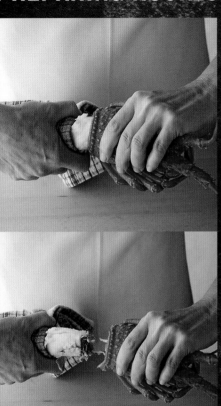

1

Hold the head in one hand and tail in the other, with a tea towel wrapped around the tail to protect your hand.

2

Twist off and discard the head.

3

Lay the tail on a chopping board on its back and press gently to flatten. Cut down both sides of the underside of the tail shell using kitchen scissors.

4

Peel the shell back.

5

Holding the tail firmly, pull the meat carefully out of the shell; the digestive tract should stay behind, attached to the tail fin.

6

Trim off the end of the meat, discarding any discoloured flesh. To halve rocklobsters, see Preparing bugs method, opposite.

PREPARING BUGS

Live bugs should be humanely killed before you prepare them as below; see page 179 for details.

1 Using a cook's knife, cut the bug in half from the head through to the tail (if this is difficult with a large bug, cut from the centre point through the head, then turn the bug 180 degrees and cut from the centre through the tail).

2 Remove the digestive tract that runs through the centre of the meat.

3 Lift the meat out of the shell. To keep the meat in one piece, see Preparing rocklobsters method, opposite.

FRESHWATER CRAYFISH (MARRONS, YABBIES AND REDCLAWS) CAN BE PREPARED IN THE SAME WAY AS BUGS AND ROCKLOBSTERS. SCAMPI CAN ALSO BE SPLIT LIKE BUGS.

STIR-FRIED BLUE SWIMMER CRABS WITH BEAN THREAD NOODLES

Recipe by
Mark Jensen

In this dish, Mark Jensen uses blue swimmer crabs, one of the few crabs that are available uncooked but already dead – which makes preparing them much easier for the novice cook. Australian crabmeat is available frozen from good fishmongers; if unavailable, add a couple of extra crabs and let the diners pick their own meat. Bean thread noodles, also known as cellophane noodles, glass noodles or Chinese vermicelli, are usually made from mung bean starch. They're very easy to use, as all you have to do is soak them in cold water until they're soft, then add them to the dish.

Soak the bean thread noodles in cold water for 15 minutes, then place them in a colander.

To make the oyster and sesame sauce, stir the ingredients together until the sugar dissolves. Set aside.

Twist off the crabs' legs and cut front legs into two pieces through the elbow. Lay the body flat on the chopping board and cut into quarters.

Heat a wok over medium heat and add the oil. When hot, add the onion and cook for a minute or so, until it starts to colour. Add the garlic and ginger and cook for another minute. Stir in the crab pieces, the oyster and sesame sauce and half of the chicken stock or water. Cover and cook for 3 minutes. If the stock has evaporated a little, top it up to its original level, then add the bean thread noodles, mushrooms and sugar snap peas. Stir-fry for about 2 minutes until the stock reduces; there should be enough sauce to moisten the dish, but it should not be soupy. Add the bean sprouts, crabmeat and most of the basil and stir-fry for a further minute. Add the lemon juice, salt and pepper.

Serve garnished with peanuts, chilli and the remaining basil. Give diners crab crackers and picks to help extract all the meat.

SERVES 4

150 g dried bean thread noodles

4 green (raw) blue swimmer crabs, cleaned (see page 180)

2 tablespoons peanut oil

¼ brown onion, halved and broken into layers

2 cloves garlic, minced

1 teaspoon minced ginger

200 ml Chicken stock (see Basics) or water

150 g oyster mushrooms, cut into bite-sized pieces

150 g sugar snap peas, trimmed and washed

100 g bean sprouts, tailed

300 g cooked crabmeat, checked for cartilage and well drained (see page 179)

1 handful Thai basil leaves

1½ tablespoons strained lemon juice

salt flakes and freshly ground white pepper, to taste

3 tablespoons roasted peanuts, roughly chopped

2 small red chillies, thinly sliced

Oyster & sesame sauce

½ cup (125 ml) oyster sauce (see Chefs' ingredients)

3 tablespoons boiling water

2 teaspoons sesame oil

2 teaspoons white sugar

ALTERNATIVE SPECIES:
marron; mud crab; prawn

Recipe by
Cheong Liew

MAMAK MUD CRAB

SERVES 6

3 × 1.5 kg live mud crabs

½ cup (125 ml) peanut oil

6 red shallots, sliced

3 cloves garlic, sliced

1 teaspoon poppy seeds

1½ cups (375 ml) coconut cream
(see Basics)

½ small pineapple, peeled and diced

½ teaspoon salt flakes

steamed basmati rice, for serving

Chilli paste

1 tablespoon cayenne pepper

2 tablespoons ground coriander

1 teaspoon ground turmeric

Spice paste

2 star anise

2 cm piece cinnamon stick, broken

2 cloves

8 red shallots, roughly chopped

4 cloves garlic, peeled

2.5 cm piece ginger, roughly chopped

3 brown cardamom pods, seeds only

2 green cardamom pods, seeds only

½ small coconut, grated

½ teaspoon salt flakes

ALTERNATIVE SPECIES:
blue swimmer crab; bug; marron; prawn; rocklobster

Cheong Liew served this dish as part of a special dinner held at the Grange Restaurant in Adelaide on 31 December 1999, to see in the new millennium. Later, he taught it at the Seafood School. *Mamak*, the Tamil word for uncle, refers to the southern Indian Muslims of Malaysia and their cuisine. Mud crabs are a bit fiddly to work with as they have to be bought live, but the large sweet chunks of meat they contain make them well worth the trouble. Bethonga pineapples are ideal for this dish, as they're smaller and sweeter than other pineapples.

Place the crabs in the freezer for 30–60 minutes, until they are insensible (see page 179).

Meanwhile, to make the chilli paste, mix all the ingredients with enough water to form a smooth paste. Set aside.

To make the spice paste, place the star anise, cinnamon and cloves in a mortar and pound with a pestle until roughly ground. Add the remaining ingredients and pound to a coarse paste. Set aside.

Bring a large saucepan of salted water to a rapid boil. Add a chilled crab, cover to return to the boil as quickly as possible, then plunge it into a bowl of iced water. Repeat with the remaining crabs, one at a time. When the crabs are cool enough to handle, clean them (see page 180), then cut the body into quarters, separate the legs, and remove and crack the claws. Reserve the top shell to cook with the crab for decoration if you wish.

Heat a wok over medium heat and add the oil. When hot, add the shallot and garlic and cook for a minute or so, until lightly browned. Add the chilli paste and fry for a minute or two, until fragrant. Add the spice paste and poppy seeds and fry for a few minutes, until fragrant, adding a little of the coconut cream to prevent the ingredients from sticking. Add the crab claws and stir-fry for a minute, then add the remaining crab and stir-fry for a few minutes until well coated with the paste. Add the remaining coconut cream and bring to the boil. Reduce the heat and add the pineapple and salt. Simmer, covered, for 3 minutes, then cook uncovered for a few more minutes, until the crab shell is red all over and most of the sauce has evaporated.

Serve with steamed basmati rice.

Recipe by
Christine Manfield

BLACK PEPPER SOFT-SHELL CRABS WITH GREEN CHILLI DIPPING SAUCE

SERVES 4

4 soft-shell crabs

vegetable oil, for deep-frying

2 tablespoons plain flour

2 tablespoons rice flour

2 teaspoons salt flakes

2 teaspoons freshly cracked black pepper

2 egg whites, lightly beaten

Green chilli dipping sauce

2 cloves garlic, peeled

2 small green chillies, halved

1 tablespoon caster sugar,
more or less, to taste

2½ tablespoons strained lime juice,
more or less, to taste

2 tablespoons fish sauce (see Chefs'
ingredients), more or less, to taste

2 tablespoons shredded coriander

ALTERNATIVE SPECIES:
*bug; prawn; redclaw; yabby (all peeled);
squid (cleaned)*

All crabs shed their shells from time to time as they grow, and it takes a couple of hours for the new shell to harden; during this time they're edible shell-and-all. Any crab can be 'soft-shell', but some are more commonly sold this way. On the east coast of the USA, soft-shell blue crabs have long been considered a delicacy. Christine Manfield presented this dish at the Seafood School when blue swimmer and mud crabs first started being raised in Queensland for sale as soft-shell crabs. They're kept in tanks monitored by robotics that detect when they've just moulted, then they're removed from the water to stop the recalcification of their shells.

To make the dipping sauce, place the garlic and chilli in a mortar and crush with a pestle, gradually working in the sugar, lime juice and fish sauce until the flavours are balanced. Stir in the coriander.

Peel off the top shells of the crabs, from back to front, and pull off and discard the gills (see page 180). Using kitchen scissors, snip the crabs in half down the centre.

Preheat the oil to 180°C (see page 61). Meanwhile, combine the plain flour, rice flour, salt and pepper. Immerse the crab in the egg white, then roll in the flour, shaking off any excess.

Carefully lower the crab pieces, a few at a time, into the oil and deep-fry for about 2 minutes, until crisp and cooked through. Remove from the oil using a slotted spoon and drain on paper towel.

Serve the crabs with the green chilli dipping sauce.

Recipe by
Damien Pignolet

CRAB & SORREL OMELETTE

SERVES 2

1 handful sorrel leaves, without stem, finely shredded

a knife tip of crushed garlic

3 tablespoons pouring cream

salt flakes and freshly ground white pepper, to taste

2 eggs

2 egg yolks

50 g cooked spanner crabmeat, checked for cartilage and well drained (see page 179)

10 g unsalted butter

ALTERNATIVE SPECIES:
prawn; redclaw (all peeled, deveined and chopped); scampi; yabby; blue swimmer crabmeat

To make a really successful omelette, Damien Pignolet says you need a small (about 22 cm), shallow-sided, pressed-steel frying pan that's reserved just for omelettes. To season the pan before you use it for the first time, heat it until it's very hot, add a little butter and wait until it turns brown, then rub the pan vigorously with a wad of paper towel to wipe it out; repeat this process. After you've made your omelette, don't ever wash the pan — just wipe it out with damp paper towel. This will ensure a non-stick surface; you could also use a non-stick pan. Sorrel is a herb with long green leaves and a lovely lemony tang; you can substitute spinach if it's unavailable. Australian spanner crabmeat from Queensland and northern New South Wales, is available frozen from good fishmongers.

Put the sorrel, garlic and 2 tablespoons of the cream into a small saucepan and cook over low heat for a minute or so, until it reduces to a light puree. Stir in salt and pepper and set aside.

Stir the eggs, egg yolks and remaining cream together, then stir in the crabmeat and a little salt and pepper.

Heat an omelette pan over medium–high heat, then add the butter and heat until melted but not coloured. Pour in the egg mixture. Shake the pan gently, then tilt it and, using a spatula, lift up the cooked section so the raw egg mixture can run underneath. Fold in the edges slightly to give an oval shape, then fold one side of the omelette over on top of the other.

Holding the pan handle underneath in one hand and a warmed plate in the other, slide the omelette out of the pan onto the plate.

Pour the sorrel sauce over the top of the omelette and serve immediately.

PRAWN PLUMS

Cheong Liew often served these delicious bites as finger food when he was at the Grange Restaurant in Adelaide. The prickly ash tree produces Sichuan peppercorns, a spice native to the Chinese region of Sichuan that has a strange tingling, numbing effect. Cheong uses the name of the tree for the salty spice mixture that is the traditional 'salt and pepper' seasoning used in many Chinese dishes. Fresh bean curd skin is available from Asian grocery stores. It doesn't need to be refrigerated but does dry out quickly once opened, so keep it in its plastic bag until you are ready to use it or it will become too brittle for this recipe. Chinese rose wine is also available from Asian grocery stores, but you can leave it out if unavailable. You'll need kitchen string and an electric mixer fitted with a beating paddle for this recipe.

To make the prickly ash, combine the Sichuan peppercorns and salt flakes in a frying pan (without oil) and heat until the salt turns light golden and the mixture smells aromatic. Transfer to a mortar and grind with a pestle to form a powder. The prickly ash will keep in an airtight jar for a month or two and makes a great seasoning for all sorts of fried foods.

Sprinkle the carrot lightly with salt and place it in a strainer for 5 minutes, then squeeze out as much liquid as possible and set the carrot aside.

Meanwhile, to make the seasoning mixture, combine all the ingredients. Set aside.

Place the prawn, pork, eggs, tapioca starch, spring onion, ginger and seasoning mixture in the bowl of an electric mixer fitted with a beating paddle. Beat the mixture for about 20 minutes until it is very well combined and quite sticky. Fold in the carrot, coriander and water chestnut.

Trim a sheet of bean curd skin into a large rectangle. Place a sheet of plastic wrap, a little larger than the bean curd skin, on a work surface. Place the bean curd skin in the centre of the plastic. Spread a strip of the prawn mixture along the longest edge of the bean curd skin, leaving several centimetres at either end (as the filling will move outwards when you tie the balls). Roll the filling firmly in the bean curd skin to create a 3 cm-wide log. Wrap tightly in the plastic wrap, twisting the ends to secure. Repeat with the remaining bean curd skin and prawn mixture. Starting in the middle of each log, use kitchen string to tie the logs tightly at 2 cm intervals to create small plum shapes.

Place the prawn logs in a steamer basket and steam over boiling water for 7 minutes. Meanwhile, preheat the oil to 180°C (see page 61).

Cut along the side of the string to form separate balls, and discard the string and plastic wrap. Place the prawn balls on a plate and cover with plastic wrap to prevent them drying out.

In batches, carefully lower the balls into the oil and deep-fry for 30 seconds, then remove and drain on paper towel. When all the balls have been fried once, repeat the frying, this time leaving them in the oil for a few minutes, until crisp and dark golden.

Sprinkle with prickly ash, squeeze over some lemon juice and serve.

Recipe by
Cheong Liew

MAKES 30–40 PIECES

3 tablespoons grated carrot

salt flakes, to taste

1.1 kg green (raw) prawns, peeled and deveined (see page 181), cut into 1.5 cm dice

150 g minced pork belly

2 eggs

40 g tapioca starch

2 spring onions (scallions), white part only, finely chopped

2 teaspoons finely chopped ginger

2 teaspoons chopped coriander

150 g water chestnuts, cut into 1 cm dice

3 sheets fresh bean curd skin

peanut oil, for deep-frying

½ lemon

Prickly ash

1½ tablespoons Sichuan peppercorns

1½ tablespoons salt flakes

Seasoning mixture

1 teaspoon salt flakes

2 teaspoons white sugar

2 teaspoons oyster sauce (see Chefs' ingredients)

¼ teaspoon freshly ground white pepper

½ teaspoon sesame oil

1 drop Chinese rose wine

ALTERNATIVE SPECIES:
crabmeat

Recipe by
Alex Kearns

PRAWN BISQUE

SERVES 6 AS AN ENTRÉE

100 ml extra virgin olive oil,
or more if needed

1 white onion, finely chopped

2 carrots, finely chopped

1 bulb fennel, thinly sliced

1 head of garlic, halved

1 tablespoon fennel seeds, lightly crushed

1 tablespoon white sugar

salt flakes and freshly ground
black pepper, to taste

500 g prawn heads and shells

1 cup (250 ml) dry white wine

750 g very ripe tomatoes, chopped

½ bunch thyme

pinch of saffron threads

crusty bread, for serving

ALTERNATIVE SPECIES:
crab; marron; redclaw; rocklobster; yabby

Nothing goes to waste in a commercial kitchen and chefs often turn what we think of as scraps into another tasty dish. You don't need prawn meat to make a delicious prawn bisque — all the flavour is in the heads and shells. So next time you peel prawns, freeze the heads and shells until you're ready to whip up this delicious bisque, which has been a favourite on Glebe Point Diner's menu since Alex Kearns opened the restaurant in 2007. When cooking the heads and shells, take your time and fry them until you get a sweet caramel aroma. This gives the bisque its richness and flavour as well as its lovely pink-orange colour. For the best result when making this recipe you'll need a mouli food mill; if you don't have one, pass the soup through a fine sieve, pressing down firmly with a ladle to extract as much liquid as possible.

Heat a saucepan over low heat and add the oil. When hot, add the onion, carrot, sliced fennel, garlic and fennel seeds and cook for 5–7 minutes, until the vegetables are soft and beginning to colour.

Stir in the sugar, salt and pepper and continue cooking until golden. Add the prawn heads and shells and, using a heavy wooden spoon, crush them well to release their juices and flavour. Cook until they turn a deep red colour, stirring and crushing often, and adding a little more oil if needed; they should keep sizzling. Add the wine, 1 litre of water, tomatoes, thyme and saffron. Bring to the boil, then reduce the heat and simmer for 40 minutes.

Pass through a mouli food mill or fine sieve into a clean saucepan, discarding the solids. Reheat over low heat; if the bisque seems a little thin, boil it until it's reduced to your desired consistency.

Ladle into bowls and serve with crusty bread.

Recipe by
Anil Ashokan

PRAWNS KERALA-STYLE

SERVES 6

50 g (golf-ball-sized piece) tamarind pulp

salt flakes, to taste

1 teaspoon ground turmeric

48 green (raw) prawns, peeled and
deveined, tails intact (see page 181)

2 tablespoons vegetable oil

1 teaspoon brown mustard seeds

10 curry leaves

14 golden shallots, thinly sliced

4 cloves garlic, thinly sliced

5 cm piece ginger, sliced into very fine strips

4 small green chillies, seeded
and sliced into strips

2 tablespoons ground coriander

1 cup (250 ml) coconut cream (see Basics)

1 bunch coriander, leaves picked

steamed basmati rice, for serving

lime cheeks, for serving

Kachumber

2 red onions, diced

2 vine-ripened tomatoes, diced

½ Lebanese cucumber, diced

3 stems coriander, leaves picked

2 tablespoons roasted peanuts, crushed

salt flakes, to taste

squeeze of lime juice

ALTERNATIVE SPECIES:
loligo squid; blue-eye trevalla; ling

Anil Ashokan was born in the state of Kerala, a coastal strip in south-western India with a cuisine rich in seafood. This prawn curry is one of the classic dishes he remembers from his childhood. The name of the accompanying salad, *kachumber* (sometimes written as *cuchumber* or *cachoombar*), means 'to cut into small pieces'; this refreshing side dish varies from region to region, with ingredients sliced or diced, sometimes dressed with lime juice and sometimes with seasoned yoghurt. It's a great accompaniment to any spicy food. Tamarind pulp is available from Asian grocery stores.

To make the kachumber, combine all the ingredients and toss to mix well. Refrigerate until you are ready to serve.

Mix the tamarind pulp with 3 tablespoons of warm water and leave it to soak for 10 minutes. Pass it through a fine sieve into a large bowl, pressing down to extract as much tamarind as possible. Add salt and half the ground turmeric to the bowl, then the prawns, stirring to coat them well. Set aside at room temperature to marinate for a few minutes.

Meanwhile, heat a frying pan and add the oil. When hot, add the mustard seeds. As they begin to crackle, add the curry leaves, then the shallots and garlic. Add the ginger and chilli and stir for a minute, until aromatic but not coloured. Stir in the ground coriander and remaining turmeric and cook for a further minute. Add the prawns with the marinade and stir to coat well, then add the coconut cream, half the coriander leaves and salt. Bring to a gentle boil, then reduce the heat and simmer gently for 3–5 minutes, until the prawns are just cooked through.

Top with the remaining coriander leaves and serve with steamed basmati rice, kachumber and lime cheeks.

Recipe by
Dan Hong

PRAWN CEVICHE WITH FENNEL, BLACK FUNGUS, KIM CHI & TIGER'S MILK

SERVES 6 AS AN ENTRÉE

18 sashimi-grade green (raw) prawns, peeled and deveined (see page 181)

1 bulb baby fennel, shaved using a mandoline (see page 77)

150 g fresh black fungus, hard parts discarded, cut into bite-sized pieces

100 g kim chi, roughly chopped

1 bunch coriander, leaves picked, stalks and roots reserved

extra virgin olive oil, for drizzling

salt flakes, to taste

puffed wild rice, for garnishing (see recipe introduction)

Tiger's milk

½ bulb fennel, roughly chopped

coriander stalks and roots reserved from above, roughly chopped

1½ green tomatoes, roughly chopped

½ telegraph (long) cucumber, roughly chopped

1 golden shallot, roughly chopped

½ long green chilli, roughly chopped

1 clove garlic, roughly chopped

finely grated zest and strained juice of 1 lime

2 teaspoons salt flakes

1½ tablespoons extra virgin olive oil

fish sauce (see Chefs' ingredients), to taste

1 tablespoon caster sugar, more or less, to taste

ALTERNATIVE SPECIES:
cuttlefish; saucer scallop; snapper

Australia has some of the most pristine waters and freshest seafood in the world, so it makes perfect sense to enjoy it as naturally as possible. Dan Hong often presents raw seafood dishes, such as this take on ceviche, at the Seafood School. Ceviche is a South American dish of raw seafood in a citrus marinade called *leche de tigre* (tiger's milk); the acid in the citrus juice alters the protein of the seafood, making it appear cooked. Just remember that when eating seafood raw, you must always buy sashimi-grade (see page 15). Kim chi, spicy Korean preserved cabbage, is available from Asian grocery stores. To make puffed wild rice, deep-fry wild rice in very hot vegetable oil – it will puff up almost immediately – then drain it on paper towel. When cool, it can be stored in an airtight container in the cupboard for weeks; it adds a great crunch to salads or other dishes.

To make the tiger's milk, combine all the ingredients except the fish sauce and sugar in a blender and process to a smooth liquid. Cover with plastic wrap and set aside for 1 hour at room temperature. Pass through a fine sieve, pressing down with the bottom of a ladle to extract as much liquid as possible. Add the fish sauce and sugar; it should be salty, sour and a little bit sweet. Refrigerate until needed.

Halve the prawns lengthways and blanch them in boiling salted water for 5 seconds, then immediately plunge them into iced water to cool. Dry on paper towel.

Place the prawns in a bowl with the fennel, black fungus, kim chi and coriander leaves. Drizzle with oil, sprinkle with salt and toss well to combine.

Divide the prawn mixture among six bowls. Ladle the tiger's milk on top to form a 'pool' around it, then drizzle oil around the dish and garnish with puffed wild rice. Serve immediately.

PRAWN COCKTAIL WITH PRAWN TOAST

Recipe by
Warren Turnbull

Who could resist this clever dish, with its combination of two classic seafood dishes – prawn cocktail and Chinese prawn toast? It's certainly a favourite at Warren Turnbull's District Dining. Of course you can use these recipes to prepare just one, but the cold cocktail and hot toast together are a taste sensation.

To make the cocktail sauce, combine all the ingredients. Set aside in the fridge.

To make the prawn toast, place the prawns in a blender and blitz for 10 seconds. Add the egg white, salt, parsley, chives, lemon zest and cayenne and blitz for a further 10 seconds. Spread the mixture evenly over one side of the bread slices, right to the edges. Lightly beat the egg yolk with a splash of water in a shallow bowl. Place the breadcrumbs in a second shallow bowl. Dip the bread, prawn-side down, into the egg yolk, then into the breadcrumbs. Cut the crusts off the bread and cut each slice into three.

Preheat the vegetable oil to 180°C (see page 61).

Meanwhile, to make the prawn cocktail, dress the cooked prawns with a little oil and salt. Divide the lettuce and avocado among plates and drizzle generously with the cocktail sauce. Drape the cooked prawns over the lettuce.

Carefully lower the bread, prawn-side down, into the oil and deep-fry for a few minutes, until golden, then turn and fry the other side. Drain on paper towel, sprinkle with salt and add a squeeze of lemon juice.

Place the hot prawn toasts alongside the prawn cocktail. Garnish with chives and serve with lemon wedges.

ALTERNATIVE SPECIES:
marron; redclaw; yabby

SERVES 6 AS AN ENTRÉE

12 cooked prawns, peeled and deveined, heads and tails intact (see page 181)

extra virgin olive oil, for drizzling

salt flakes, to taste

1 iceberg lettuce, cut into 12 wedges

1 large avocado, peeled and cut into 12 wedges

6 chives

lemon wedges, to serve

Cocktail sauce

1 cup (300 g) whole-egg mayonnaise

1 tablespoon tomato ketchup

1 teaspoon brandy

1 teaspoon Worcestershire sauce

3 drops of Tabasco sauce

5 chives, finely snipped

1 stem French tarragon (see Chefs' ingredients), leaves picked and finely chopped

juice of ½ lemon, strained

salt flakes, to taste

Prawn toast

700 g green (raw) prawns, peeled and deveined (see page 181)

1 egg, separated

salt flakes, to taste

1 stem flat-leaf parsley leaves, chopped

5 chives, finely snipped

finely grated zest of ¼ lemon

pinch of cayenne pepper

4 slices white sandwich bread

½ cup (50 g) packaged breadcrumbs

vegetable oil, for frying

squeeze of lemon juice

Recipe by
Pete Evans

GARLIC PRAWNS

SERVES 6

3 tablespoons extra virgin olive oil

12 cloves garlic, thinly sliced

4 anchovy fillets in oil (see Chefs' ingredients), drained

4 tablespoons chopped flat-leaf parsley

24 green (raw) prawns, peeled and deveined, tails intact (see page 181)

800 g tinned whole peeled tomatoes, drained and crushed in the hand

salt flakes and freshly ground black pepper, to taste

2 thick slices ciabatta, toasted and torn into pieces

Chilli confit

1 cup (100 g) seeded and chopped long red chillies

1 cup (250 ml) olive oil

ALTERNATIVE SPECIES:
redclaw; scampi; yabby

Who doesn't love garlic prawns? This version by keen fisherman and chef Pete Evans shows just how easy they are to prepare, while also adding some clever touches such as toasted ciabatta to soak up all the delicious garlicky sauce. The chilli confit recipe makes more than you'll need for this dish, but it keeps refrigerated for a few weeks and is great to add a chilli kick to any dish. Of course, you could just use a little chopped fresh chilli or dried chilli flakes if you prefer.

To make the chilli confit, place the chilli and oil in a small saucepan over the lowest heat possible (the oil should be just past warm) for about 2 hours until the chilli is soft. Cool, then store in a sterilised, airtight jar and refrigerate.

Place the oil, garlic and anchovies in a cold frying pan and cook over medium heat until the garlic just starts to turn golden. Add 3 tablespoons of the chilli confit, together with the parsley and prawns and toss for 20 seconds. Add the tomatoes, salt and pepper and cook for a few minutes, until the prawns just turn opaque. Add the bread and allow it to soak up the sauce, then serve immediately.

Recipe by
Mark Best

DEEP-FRIED
SCHOOL PRAWNS

SERVES 6 AS AN ENTRÉE

200 g tapioca starch

1 teaspoon fine sea salt

1 teaspoon freshly ground white pepper

vegetable oil, for deep-frying

900 g small green (raw) school prawns

1 teaspoon Spanish smoked hot paprika
(see Chefs' ingredients)

1 teaspoon salt flakes

lemon wedges, for serving

ALTERNATIVE SPECIES:
sandy sprat; whitebait

For all his kitchen wizardry, it's a treat when Mark Best presents a dish as simple as this, something he whips up at home to serve with drinks. School prawns, which are usually available from about October to March, are often sold small enough to be eaten head and all. Choose the smallest and freshest possible; they should have a fresh sea smell and no discolouration of the head. If they are a little large, remove the heads before cooking and allow twice as many prawns.

Sift the tapioca flour, fine salt and pepper together.

Preheat the oil to 190°C (see page 61). Toss the prawns with the seasoned flour until well coated, then place them in a colander and shake off any excess flour.

Fry the prawns, in batches, for a couple of minutes until golden. Remove and drain on paper towel. Remember to allow the oil temperature to recover between batches.

Dust the prawns with paprika and salt flakes. Serve with lemon wedges and eat while piping hot.

SEAFOOD MEZE

Whether it's tapas, antipasto, yum cha or meze, small plates of shared food are a great way to eat. You try a lot of different flavours, everyone takes as little or as much as they like, and it brings us back to one of the main reasons we sit at the table together – to share each other's company. The tradition of meze (or mezze) is found all over the Middle East, as well as in North Africa, Greece and Turkey, sometimes in its traditional role of snacks to have with a drink (very similar to tapas) and sometimes as an elaborate first course. Some of the best meze in Sydney is found at Turkish restaurant Efendy, whose owner-chef, Somer Sivrioglu, presented this selection at the Seafood School.

Kataifi (or kadayif) is a finely shredded pastry available from the chiller section of some delis. Isot pepper is mild Turkish chilli flakes; if unavailable use any dried chilli flakes, though you may need to reduce the quantity. Biber salçasi is Turkish paprika or capsicum paste; if unavailable, puree 2 teaspoons of tomato paste with half a roasted capsicum. Isot pepper and biber salçasi are both available from Turkish grocery stores. Serve the meze with plenty of pide or flatbread and some raki, or ouzo, if you like. Of course, you could serve just one of these dishes as an entrée, but to serve all three dishes at once, first make the accompaniments, then get all the seafood ready to cook. While the prawns are in the oven, grill the sardines and fry the mussels.

KADAYIF-WRAPPED PRAWNS WITH MUHAMMARA

Remove the kataifi pastry from the fridge 1 hour before using, to allow it to soften.

To make the muhammara, preheat the oven to 200°C (fan-forced). Place the garlic on an oiled baking tray and cook for about 5 minutes, until soft. Meanwhile, place the capsicums on a hot grill and cook until blackened all over. Place the capsicums in a bowl and cover with plastic wrap. When the capsicums are cool enough to handle, peel and discard the skin, seeds and membrane. Chop finely. Place the roasted garlic and walnuts in a mortar and crush with a pestle to form a paste. Transfer to a bowl and mix in the capsicum, isot pepper, biber salçasi, lemon juice, pomegranate molasses and enough oil to form a thick paste. Refrigerate until needed; bring back to room temperature before serving.

Place a baking tray in the oven and preheat to 200°C (fan-forced). Combine the ghee with the orange juice and zest and salt, then drizzle this over the kataifi pastry to loosen it up. Gently separate the pastry into six pieces and place each piece in a long thin strip on a work surface. Place a prawn at one end of each piece. Tuck the end of the pastry into the tail shell to secure it and roll the pastry around the prawn, working towards the head, ensuring you have a thin, even layer of pastry (you may not need all of it). Place the prawns on the baking tray and cook for 5–8 minutes, until the pastry is crisp and slightly coloured and the prawns are just opaque.

To serve, spread the muhammara on a platter and place the prawns, tail up, on top. Garnish with sumac. >

Recipe by
Somer Sivrioglu

SERVES 6 AS AN ENTRÉE

KADAYIF-WRAPPED PRAWNS WITH MUHAMMARA

50 g fresh kataifi (kadayif) pastry

3 teaspoons ghee, melted

2 teaspoons strained orange juice

¼ teaspoon finely grated orange zest

salt flakes, to taste

6 large green (raw) prawns, peeled and deveined, tails intact (see page 181)

sumac, for garnishing

Muhammara (Walnut capsicum dip)

4 cloves garlic, peeled

2 red capsicums (peppers)

200 g walnuts, finely chopped

2 teaspoons isot pepper

50 g sweet biber salçasi

strained juice of ½ lemon

2 tablespoons pomegranate molasses

extra virgin olive oil, for forming a paste

ALTERNATIVE SPECIES:
marron; redclaw; scampi; yabby

SARDINES WRAPPED IN VINE LEAVES

SARDINES WRAPPED IN VINE LEAVES

12 small Australian sardines, butterflied
(see page 13), skin on and fins trimmed off

12 preserved vine leaves,
 soaked in water for 1 hour

2 tablespoons finely chopped
flat-leaf parsley

2 tablespoons finely chopped mint

2 cloves garlic, finely chopped

2 tablespoons finely chopped pine nuts

2 tablespoons currants

1 tablespoon strained lemon juice

extra virgin olive oil, for drizzling

pomegranate molasses, for serving

pomegranate seeds, for serving

ALTERNATIVE SPECIES:
garfish; very small red mullet

Preheat a barbecue or char-grill pan over high heat. Check the fish for any remaining scales. Pat the vine leaves dry and spread out on a work surface, shiny-side down. Combine the parsley, mint, garlic, pine nuts, currants and lemon juice. Place a small spoonful in the centre of each sardine, then close the fish over the stuffing and place on a vine leaf. Roll the sardines tightly in the vine leaves, tucking in the ends to completely enclose the fish. Drizzle with oil and grill for 2–3 minutes each side, until the leaf is coloured and slightly crisp.

Arrange the wrapped sardines on a plate and serve with a drizzle of pomegranate molasses and a scattering of pomegranate seeds.

BEER-BATTERED MUSSELS WITH TARATOR

30 blue mussels, scrubbed (see page 121)

1½ cups (225 g) plain flour

165 ml lager beer

1 egg, separated

vegetable oil, for shallow-frying

salt flakes and freshly ground
black pepper, to taste

Tarator (Walnut sauce)

3 slices day-old white sandwich
bread, crusts removed

100 ml milk

1½ cups (150 g) walnuts

2 cloves garlic, peeled

1 teaspoon salt flakes

½ cup (125 ml) extra virgin olive oil

2 tablespoons white wine vinegar
(see Chefs' ingredients)

juice of 1 lemon, strained

ALTERNATIVE SPECIES:
commercial scallop; oyster

To make the tarator, soak the bread in the milk for 5 minutes, then squeeze to remove excess liquid. Finely chop the walnuts in a food processor, then place them in a bowl. Add the bread and knead to combine. Crush the garlic and salt with the flat of a knife to form a paste. Stir the oil, vinegar, lemon juice and crushed garlic into the walnut mixture. Cover and refrigerate for at least 1 hour. Return to room temperature and stir well before serving, as it may separate. If refrigerating overnight, mix in a drizzle of extra virgin olive oil to loosen it up just before serving.

Place the mussels in a bowl and cover them with boiling water. Using a blunt knife (such as a butter knife), open the shells along the broad edge and remove the mussels. Snip off the beards and place the mussels on paper towel to drain. Place ½ cup (75 g) of flour in a bowl, pour in the beer and egg yolk and mix well. Whisk the egg white until it forms soft peaks and fold into the flour mixture. Heat the oil in a frying pan over medium–high heat. Add the salt and pepper to the remaining flour. Toss the mussels in the flour, shaking off any excess, then dip them in the batter. Working in batches, lower the battered mussels carefully into the oil and fry for a minute or so until dark golden brown on both sides. Drain on paper towel.

To serve, arrange the beer-battered mussels in a bowl with the tarator alongside for dipping.

Recipe by
Matt Moran

SCAMPI IN BRIK PASTRY WITH AÏOLI & GREMOLATA

SERVES 6 AS AN ENTRÉE

12 pieces brik pastry

12 green (raw) scampi, peeled and deveined, tails intact (see page 181)

vegetable oil, for deep-frying

1 egg, lightly beaten

4 tablespoons Aïoli (see Basics)

1 tablespoon strained lemon juice

1 tablespoon snipped celery cress (see Chefs' ingredients)

Gremolata

½ bunch flat-leaf parsley, leaves picked

½ clove garlic

2½ tablespoons olive oil

salt flakes and freshly ground black pepper, to taste

ALTERNATIVE SPECIES:
large prawn

Scampi are delicate, sweet and delicious, and this recipe, which is often on Matt Moran's menu at ARIA, is an excellent, no-fuss way to serve them. Brik pastry is a fine Tunisian pastry similar to filo pastry. It's sold in some delis and Middle Eastern grocers, but you can substitute filo if it's unavailable.

To make the gremolata, combine all the ingredients and use a stick blender to chop finely. Set aside at room temperature.

Pass the pastry through a linguine cutter on a pasta machine to make thin strips about 5 mm wide, or roll it up into a log and carefully slice it by hand. Wrap each scampi in the strips of pastry, brushing the ends with egg to help stick them together.

Preheat the oil to 180°C (see page 61). Working in batches, carefully lower the scampi into the oil and deep-fry for 1–2 minutes, until golden brown. Drain on paper towel.

To serve, place a spoonful of aïoli in the centre of each plate and top with two scampi. Stir the lemon juice through the gremolata and drizzle it around the plates. Garnish with celery cress.

Recipe by
David Thompson

SALAD OF ROCKLOBSTER & POMELO

SERVES 6 AS AN ENTRÉE

1 × 1 kg live rocklobster

8 large pomelo segments,
broken into small pieces

4 stalks lemongrass, white part only,
very finely chopped

4 red shallots, sliced

1 large handful mint leaves

1 large handful coriander leaves

6 cloves garlic, thinly sliced and deep-fried

8 red shallots, extra, thinly sliced
and deep-fried

Thai dressing

4 coriander roots, scraped

1 large red chilli, seeded
and roughly chopped

a few scud chillies (see page 140)

good pinch of salt flakes

3–4 tablespoons caster sugar, to taste

⅔ cup (160 ml) strained lime juice,
more or less, to taste

4 tablespoons fish sauce (see Chefs'
ingredients), more or less, to taste

ALTERNATIVE SPECIES:
*blue mussel; bug; crab; marron; prawn;
redclaw; yabby*

This is a great way to make expensive rocklobster go a long way. You can buy deep-fried garlic and shallots in Asian grocery stores, but you'll get an infinitely better result if you make your own: simply deep-fry them for a few minutes in hot vegetable oil until they turn golden, stirring with a spider to ensure they colour evenly, then drain on paper towel. Pomelo is a large thick-skinned citrus fruit; if unavailable, use green mango. To segment pomelo, use a small sharp knife to remove the skin, then cut down either side of the white membranes to release the segments. David Thompson always explains at his classes that a Thai dish such as this would traditionally be served at the same time as a number of other dishes – a curry, a stir-fry and a soup, for example – along with steamed jasmine rice.

Place the rocklobster in the freezer for 30–60 minutes, until insensible (see page 179).

Meanwhile, to make the Thai dressing, place the coriander root, large chilli, scuds and salt in a mortar and pound with a pestle until quite fine. Add the sugar, lime juice and fish sauce and stir until dissolved. Taste – it should be spicy, sour, salty and sweet; and adjust if need be.

Bring a large saucepan of salted water to a rapid boil. Add the chilled rocklobster, and cover to return to the boil as quickly as possible. Cook for 8 minutes from the time it returns to the boil, then plunge it into iced water.

Remove the meat from the shell (see page 182) and cut it into 1 cm-thick slices. Combine the rocklobster, pomelo, lemongrass, sliced shallots, mint and coriander and toss with the dressing. Serve sprinkled with the deep-fried shallots and garlic.

YABBY, ASPARAGUS & SAFFRON RISOTTO

I've never seen anyone as passionate about making risotto as Alessandro Pavoni – for him it's a religion rather than an art. The region of Lombardy, where he was born, is the home of the classic risotto Milanese, so perhaps it's not surprising. One of the things he's particular about is not stirring the risotto as soon as the liquid is added, rather letting it cook uninterrupted for about 10 minutes; once you start stirring, you mustn't stop until the risotto's ready. Alessandro's risotto is made *all'onda* (wave-like), and it's served on a flat plate or shallow bowl, not heaped into a mound. It should be soupy enough to flatten out on the plate when you tap the bottom with your hand. Once you've mastered the method, you can use whatever flavourings you like, though do use carnaroli rice – a short-grained Italian rice that gives a much better result than the more commonly used arborio. It's available from good delis and online.

Place the yabbies in the freezer for 30 minutes or so, until insensible (see page 179).

Bring a large saucepan of salted water to a rapid boil. Add the chilled yabbies, then cover to return to the boil as quickly as possible. Cook for 2 minutes from the time the yabbies go into the saucepan, then drain and place them in iced water to cool.

Peel the yabbies, reserving the heads and shells for the stock. Remove the digestive tract using a toothpick (see page 181) and pick the meat from the claws. Set aside.

To make the yabby stock, combine all the ingredients in a large saucepan. Bring to the boil, then reduce the heat and simmer for 20 minutes, skimming regularly to remove any froth that floats to the top. Remove the pan from the heat and set it aside to rest for 20 minutes at room temperature, then ladle the stock through a coffee filter or muslin-lined sieve. Transfer 1.5 litres of the stock into a clean pan and bring to a simmer, then cover and keep warm over the lowest heat. The leftover stock can be kept in an airtight container in the fridge for a few days or in the freezer for 3 months.

Soak the saffron threads in a tablespoon of warm yabby stock. Cut the asparagus spears in half, then cut the top halves of the spears lengthways into halves or quarters depending on size, and finely chop the bottom halves. Warm the wine over low heat until lukewarm.

Heat a large heavy-based frying pan over medium heat and add the oil. When hot, add the shallot and cook for 2 minutes. Add the rice, shake the pan to coat the grains in oil and stir for about 2 minutes, until quite hot. Add the wine, but do not stir; reduce the heat and shake the pan occasionally until the wine has been absorbed. Add enough yabby stock to just cover the rice. Shake the pan to combine ingredients – do not stir. Leave the rice to cook, without stirring, for 10 minutes, adding stock as necessary to keep the rice just covered and shaking the pan occasionally.

After 10 minutes, stir in the saffron with its soaking liquid and another ladle of stock. Stir continuously, adding more stock as each ladleful is absorbed. After a further 6 minutes, add the asparagus and stir for another minute.

Remove the pan from the heat, add the yabbies, butter, parsley and salt and stir vigorously. Add a little more stock if the risotto isn't quite moist enough, then set aside to rest, uncovered, for 1 minute.

Spoon the risotto evenly onto warm flat plates or shallow bowls, tapping the bottom to flatten out the risotto, and serve.

Recipe by
Alessandro Pavoni

SERVES 6

30 live yabbies

2 pinches of saffron threads

20 green asparagus spears, ends trimmed and reserved for stock

200 ml dry white wine

100 ml extra virgin olive oil

5 golden shallots, finely diced

600 g carnaroli rice

100 g unsalted butter

½ bunch flat-leaf parsley, leaves chopped

salt flakes, to taste

Yabby stock

yabby heads and shells, reserved from above

asparagus trimmings, reserved from above

1 clove garlic, crushed

1 white onion, halved

1 carrot, roughly chopped

1 leek, roughly chopped and washed

1 stalk celery, roughly chopped

2 ripe tomatoes, roughly chopped

a few parsley stalks

a few basil leaves

100 ml dry white wine

2 litres water

ALTERNATIVE SPECIES:
marron; prawn; redclaw; scampi

MARRON Á LA PARISIENNE

Shannon Bennett has been described as the *enfant terrible* of Australian haute cuisine. He certainly has shown amazing drive and dedication to perfection from a young age, and dining at Melbourne's Vue de Monde is a world-class experience. Shannon's dishes may be far from simple, but his precision carries over to his recipe writing and if you break this recipe down into its various elements and tackle them one at a time, you will end up with a superb result. Of course, you could simplify the dish by leaving out elements such as the pastis citrus jelly if you wish . . . but then it won't be Shannon's dish. Seafood prepared *á la Parisienne* (Paris-style) is usually served cold with a mayonnaise sauce and often garnished with finely chopped vegetables also in mayonnaise (such as this Russian salad), hard-boiled eggs and jelly. The jelly recipe makes more than you'll need; but it is delicious set and served with pâtés, terrines or charcuterie. It will keep refrigerated for up to 1 week.

Recipe by
Shannon Bennett

Place the marrons in the freezer for 30 minutes or so, until insensible (see page 179).

To make the pastis citrus jelly, heat a saucepan over medium heat and add the oil. When hot, add the shallot, garlic, thyme, tarragon and bay leaf and cook for about 6 minutes, until the shallot is soft and translucent. Add the pastis, Noilly Prat and orange juice, then increase the heat and boil until reduced by two-thirds. Add the fish stock and return to the boil. Reduce the heat and simmer for 20 minutes. Whisk in the egg whites and leave for 5–10 minutes to form a raft on the top of the liquid; this clarifies the jelly by trapping particles in the raft as it cooks. Remove from the heat and, using a fine mesh spider or slotted spoon, carefully lift off and discard the raft.

Soak the gelatine in a little cold water, then squeeze out any excess liquid. Ladle the jelly mixture through a muslin-lined sieve into a bowl. Add the gelatine and stir until dissolved. Set aside at room temperature, or in the fridge if in a hurry. Ensure the jelly has cooled, but is not completely set, before using.

Bring a large saucepan of salted water to a rapid boil. Add the chilled marrons, and cover to return to the boil as quickly as possible. Boil for 6 minutes, then refresh in iced water for 6 minutes. Using a serrated knife, halve the marrons lengthways, then rinse the heads to remove any impurities. Remove the claws, crack them with the back of a knife and carefully pry out the flesh. Refrigerate until needed. Remove the tail meat, discard the digestive tract (see page 181) and return the flesh to the opposite shell, turning the meat over to show the red flesh. Refrigerate until needed.

To make the Russian salad, blanch the carrot, turnip and potato in boiling salted water for about 4 minutes, until just cooked. Refresh in iced water, then drain, dry and place in a large mixing bowl. Add the shallot and mushroom and stir to combine. Heat a frying pan and add the oil. When hot, add the pancetta and cook for about 5 minutes, until crisp and well coloured. Drain and add to the vegetables with the anchovies, capers and cornichons and mix well. Slice each egg lengthways, reserving the six best slices. Chop the remainder and combine with the vegetable mixture. Mix the salad with the lemon juice, salt and pepper and enough Marie Rose mayonnaise to coat the vegetables.

Fill the head section of each shell with Russian salad. Place a slice of egg and a piece of claw meat on top. Glaze with the pastis citrus jelly and refrigerate for 5–10 minutes.

Serve with a lemon half and the remaining Marie Rose mayonnaise and Russian salad on the side.

ALTERNATIVE SPECIES:
redclaw; rocklobster; scampi; yabby

SERVES 6

6 × 350 g live marrons

200 ml Pastis citrus jelly (see below), at room temperature

200 ml Marie Rose mayonnaise (see Basics)

3 small lemons, halved, wrapped in muslin

Pastis citrus jelly

2 teaspoons extra virgin olive oil

4 golden shallots, thinly sliced

1 clove garlic, thinly sliced

2 sprigs thyme

2 stems French tarragon (see Chefs' ingredients)

1 fresh bay leaf

1 cup (250 ml) pastis

1 cup (250 ml) Noilly Prat

1 cup (250 ml) strained, freshly squeezed orange juice

1.5 litres Fish stock (see Basics)

5 egg whites

6 sheets titanium-grade leaf gelatine (see page 128)

Russian salad

1 carrot, peeled and diced

1 turnip, peeled and diced

1 large desiree potato, peeled and diced

2 golden shallots, finely chopped

10 button mushrooms, diced

1 tablespoon extra virgin olive oil

6 thick slices pancetta, diced

6 anchovy fillets in oil (see Chefs' Ingredients), drained and crushed

1 tablespoon salted baby capers, rinsed and dried

2 tablespoons finely diced cornichons

2 eggs, boiled for 10 minutes

juice of ½ lemon, strained

salt flakes and freshly ground white pepper, to taste

Recipe by
Guillaume Brahimi

MORETON BAY BUGS MARINATED IN CHERMOULA WITH COUSCOUS, EGGPLANT & CAPSICUM

SERVES 4 AS AN ENTRÉE

1 eggplant (aubergine)

½ clove garlic, cut into slivers

olive oil, for brushing and pan-frying

salt flakes and freshly ground
white pepper, to taste

½ red capsicum (pepper)

250 g moghrabieh couscous

4 large green (raw) Moreton Bay bugs,
peeled and deveined (see page 183)

Chermoula

1 tablespoon cumin seeds

1 tablespoon coriander seeds

1 teaspoon chilli flakes

1 tablespoon Spanish smoked sweet paprika
(see Chefs' ingredients)

large pinch of saffron threads

1 large handful coriander leaves

1 large handful flat-leaf parsley leaves

6 cloves garlic, roughly chopped

juice of 2 lemons, strained

300 ml extra virgin olive oil

salt flakes, to taste

ALTERNATIVE SPECIES:
*Balmain bug; marron; prawn; redclaw;
rocklobster; yabby*

Moreton Bay bugs and Balmain bugs are very similar. Guillaume Brahimi uses Moreton Bay bugs in this recipe, but you could use either. They combine deliciously with the chermoula, a slightly spicy North African herb paste, and moghrabieh (sometimes called pearl or Israeli couscous), which is larger than regular couscous, like small balls of pasta. If you don't have a char-grill, roast the capsicum in the oven until well blackened. The chermoula recipe makes more than you'll need for this dish, but it will keep covered in the fridge for up to 1 week and is delicious with all sorts of seafood.

Preheat the oven to 180°C (fan-forced). Cut the eggplant in half and score the flesh. Stud the eggplant with the garlic, brush the flesh liberally with oil and sprinkle with salt and pepper. Cook in the oven for about 30 minutes, until soft. Set aside.

Meanwhile, heat a barbecue or char-grill pan and cook the capsicum until blackened. Place in a bowl and cover with plastic wrap; when cool enough to handle, peel and slice the flesh into fine strips. Set aside.

Bring a large saucepan of salted water to the boil, add the couscous and cook, according to the packet instructions until tender. Rinse under cold water and drain well.

To make the chermoula, grind the cumin, coriander, chilli flakes, paprika and saffron together in a spice grinder. Place in a food processor with the remaining ingredients and process into a paste. Brush the bugs with some of the chermoula.

Remove the flesh from the eggplant, discarding the skin, then chop finely and mix with the capsicum strips. Add the couscous and a touch of chermoula and stir to combine.

Heat a char-grill or frying pan over medium–high heat, brush with a little oil and cook the bugs for about 2 minutes on each side; they should still be slightly translucent in the centre.

Place the couscous mixture on a platter, top with the bugs and serve with chermoula on the side.

BASICS

Recipe by
Warren Turnbull

FLATBREAD

Makes 6

300 g plain flour, sifted

⅔ cup (160 ml) lukewarm water

1½ tablespoons olive oil

½ teaspoon caster sugar

½ teaspoon dried yeast

pinch of salt flakes

plain flour, extra, for dusting

This flatbread is served with Warren Turnbull's Smoked eel pâté (see page 34), but could also be used with Salmon rillettes (see page 30), Baccala Mantecato alla Veneziana (see page 29) or Seafood meze (see page 207).

Combine the flour, water, oil, sugar, yeast and salt in the bowl of an electric mixer fitted with a dough hook and knead until smooth. Cover the bowl with a clean, dry cloth and leave in a warm place for about 30 minutes, until doubled in size.

Remove the dough from the bowl and knead briefly on a lightly floured work surface to remove air bubbles. Return the dough to the bowl, then cover and set aside to rise again, until doubled in size.

Preheat the oven to 250°C (fan-forced). Place the dough on a lightly floured work surface and knead until smooth.

Divide the dough into six portions and roll into 5 mm-thick ovals. Place on an oiled baking tray and bake for 6–10 minutes, until golden. Serve warm.

Recipe by
Sydney Seafood School

CRÊPES

Makes 6 crêpes

1 cup (250 ml) milk

3 tablespoons double cream

3 eggs

¾ cup (110 g) plain flour

pinch of salt

40 g unsalted butter, melted

vegetable oil, for oiling

You'll need these crêpes to make Damien Pignolet's Coulibiac recipe (see page 42). You could also make seafood crêpes – simply fill with seafood and sauce and bake them in the oven – a great way to use up leftovers. Crêpes will keep refrigerated for several days, or frozen for up to 1 month.

Combine the milk, cream and eggs in a blender. Add the flour and salt and blend for 30 seconds, then refrigerate for 30 minutes.

Stir in the butter and strain into a jug. If the mixture is too thick, add a little more milk; it should barely coat a wooden spoon. Heat a 23–24 cm frying pan and oil it lightly. Pour in just enough batter to coat the bottom of the pan, swirling it quickly to cover the base evenly. Cook for about 30 seconds, until the edges begin to curl and the base is golden brown. Loosen the edges, then turn the crêpe with your fingers or an egg lifter and cook for another 20 seconds or so until golden and dry. Slide out of the pan onto a clean, dry cloth. Repeat with the remaining batter, stacking the cooked crêpes on top of one another.

FISH STOCK

Recipe by
Frank Camorra

Fish stock is the easiest stock to make as, unlike meat stocks, it only needs to simmer for 20 minutes. Fish heads and frames are very inexpensive, and the flavour of homemade stock is better than any commercial product. You can use the bones of any non-oily fish, although many chefs say snapper gives the best results. It's worth making a big potful and freezing the excess in small containers for up to 6 months.

Place the fish head, whole onion, whole tomato, bay leaves and garlic in a large stockpot and add 1.5 litres of cold water. Bring to the boil over high heat, then reduce the heat to low and simmer for 20 minutes, skimming regularly to remove any froth that floats to the surface. Set aside to cool, then strain the stock through a muslin-lined sieve, discarding the solids.

MAKES ABOUT 1.5 LITRES

1 large snapper head, washed to remove any blood

1 brown onion, peeled

1 tomato

2 fresh bay leaves

1 head garlic, halved

1.5 litres cold water

CHICKEN STOCK

Recipe by
Sydney Seafood School

Chicken stock is very simple and inexpensive to make – and even more versatile than fish stock. Many seafood recipes use chicken, rather than fish, stock as it has a more neutral flavour. It's a great way to add a boost to any sauce or to use as a base for soups or casseroles, and is worth having on hand in the freezer; it keeps for up to 6 months.

Bring a large saucepan of water to the boil. Plunge the chicken bones into the boiling water and return to the boil, then remove the bones and discard the water; this helps to remove impurities from the bones.

Rinse the bones in cold water. Place them into a large saucepan and cover with 3 litres of cold water. Bring to the boil, then reduce the heat and simmer for 2 hours, skimming regularly to remove any froth that floats to the surface.

Strain the stock through a muslin-lined sieve, discarding the bones. Remove any fat from the surface before using.

MAKES ABOUT 2 LITRES

2 kg chicken bones (necks, backs, wings)

3 litres cold water

Recipe by
Brent Savage

REDUCED VEAL STOCK

MAKES ABOUT 1 CUP (250 ML)

2 kg veal bones

400 ml red wine

2 tablespoons vegetable oil

2 stalks celery, chopped

1 carrot, chopped

1 brown onion, chopped

1 head garlic, halved

2 bay leaves

2 sprigs thyme

Reduced veal stock is the sort of thing chefs use to add a depth of flavour to their dishes. Although this takes a while to make, you don't need to be standing by the pan the whole time – so put it on to cook and go about your business, then when it's ready, freeze it for up to 6 months and use it to add a professional touch to your dishes.

Preheat the oven to 180°C (fan-forced). Place the bones in a roasting tin and cook in the oven for 40 minutes. Remove the bones from the oven and place them in a large saucepan. Add the red wine to the roasting tin and stir well to remove sediment. Add this to the pan.

Heat a frying pan over medium heat and add the oil. When hot, add the celery, carrot, onion, garlic, bay leaves and thyme and cook until golden. Add to the saucepan, then cover with water and bring to the boil. Reduce the heat and simmer for 2½ hours, skimming regularly to remove any froth that floats to the surface.

Ladle the stock through a fine sieve lined with muslin, discarding the solids. Return the liquid to a clean saucepan and boil until reduced to 1 cup (250 ml), skimming to remove any froth or fat that floats to the top. Pass the stock through a muslin-lined sieve as soon as it's reduced.

Recipe by
David Thompson

COCONUT CREAM & MILK

MAKES ABOUT 1 CUP (250 ML)
COCONUT CREAM

1 coconut

David Thompson insists on making fresh coconut cream and milk for curries. It's easy and infinitely better than the commercial versions. No matter how much water is added, the yield of coconut cream will always be the same, as the cream separates from the milk; using more water will just give more diluted milk. Both cream and milk are best used within a few hours of making; after this time, they'll start to sour.

Grate the coconut flesh, or prise it from the shell and chop it roughly, avoiding the brown inner skin. Process in a food processor with 1 cup (250 ml) of warm water.

Place a small quantity at a time into a piece of muslin and wring tightly over a strainer into a non-metal bowl, extracting as much liquid as possible. Leave for at least 20 minutes to separate. The cream is the thicker, opaque liquid that rises to the top of the milk (the thinner liquid on the bottom).

The coconut flesh can be mixed with warm water and squeezed again to extract more coconut milk, however there'll be very little cream in this second pressing.

AÏOLI

Recipe by
Guillaume Brahimi

Aïoli is a garlic-flavoured mayonnaise from the south of France. It takes a bit of practice to form an emulsion using a mortar and pestle; you may find it easier to put the garlic paste in a bowl and whisk in the eggs and oil. Aïoli keeps, covered and refrigerated, for a couple of days.

Place the garlic and salt in a mortar and pound with a pestle. Add the egg yolks and mix to combine. Slowly add the oil, drop by drop at first, mixing continuously to form an emulsion.

MAKES ABOUT 2 CUPS (500 ML)

6 plump cloves garlic, halved and green germ removed from the centre

2 teaspoons salt flakes

3 large egg yolks

300 ml extra virgin olive oil

TARTARE SAUCE

Recipe by
Alex Herbert

Alex Herbert adapted this tartare sauce from a recipe by English food writer Simon Hopkinson. If you don't want to make your own mayonnaise, jazz up commercial whole-egg mayonnaise with the ingredients given here.

Place the capers in a small saucepan of water. Bring to the boil, then drain and repeat. Pat dry. Chop one-third of the capers and set aside.

Combine the olive and grapeseed oils in a jug. Place the egg yolks, mustard, Tabasco sauce, vinegar and ½ teaspoon of salt in a bowl and whisk in the oils, starting slowly, one drop at a time, and ensuring that each addition is well incorporated.

Fold in the chives, tarragon, parsley, cornichons, chopped and whole capers, salt and pepper, to taste.

MAKES ABOUT 300 ML

1½ tablespoons salted capers

150 ml extra virgin olive oil

150 ml grapeseed oil

2 egg yolks

1 teaspoon Dijon mustard

4 drops of Tabasco sauce

2 teaspoons white wine vinegar (see Chefs' ingredients)

salt flakes and freshly ground black pepper, to taste

1 tablespoon snipped chives

4 stems French tarragon (see Chefs' ingredients), leaves picked and chopped

1½ tablespoons chopped flat-leaf parsley

1½ teaspoons chopped cornichons

MARIE ROSE MAYONNAISE

Recipe by
Shannon Bennett

This classic 'cocktail sauce' keeps refrigerated for a week and is delicious with any seafood or even chicken. It's important to use tomato ketchup rather than tomato sauce in this recipe.

Combine the egg yolks, mustard, vinegar, salt and pepper in a food processor. With the motor running, very slowly drizzle in the sunflower oil until half has been incorporated, then combine the remaining sunflower oil with the olive oil and drizzle in a thin stream until incorporated. Add a little warm water if the mayonnaise is too thick. Transfer to a bowl, then add the tomato ketchup, Tabasco sauce and lemon juice and whisk until well combined. Taste and add extra salt and pepper if needed. Refrigerate until required.

2 egg yolks

1 tablespoon Dijon mustard

2½ tablespoons sherry vinegar

salt flakes and freshly ground white pepper, to taste

200 ml sunflower oil

2½ tablespoons extra virgin olive oil

100 ml tomato ketchup

Tabasco sauce, to taste

squeeze of lemon juice

SEAFOOD KIT

A good-quality **FILLETING KNIFE** with a long, thin, flexible blade is perfect for removing fillets from a whole fish and for skinning fillets.

CRAB CRACKERS are the easiest way to break crab shells, both to let flavourings in when cooking and to make it easier to extract meat; nutcrackers may also be used.

FISH TWEEZERS are useful for removing the fine bones (called pin-bones) that are often left behind when fish are filleted.

An **OYSTER KNIFE** is essential if you want to shuck your own oysters – the wide, blunt blade with a pointed end is especially designed for sliding between the two shells and popping them open.

CRAB & LOBSTER PICKS are long, thin forks that are used to extract meat from the legs of crabs and rocklobsters.

CHEFS' INGREDIENTS

Ever eaten a dish in a restaurant and then been disappointed when you've made it at home and it doesn't taste as good? Often, this simply comes down to the quality of the ingredients. Premium ingredients may cost a bit more, but remember that you'll use most of these listed below in fairly small quantities, so the additional cost to the overall dish is minor — and the difference in taste can be huge!

Anchovy fillets
If available, use Ortiz anchovies. They have a much milder flavour than other brands and are also less salty.

Breadcrumbs
Instead of using shop-bought breadcrumbs, pulse day-old bread in a food processor to make fresh breadcrumbs. This is a great way to use up stale bread and you can keep the crumbs in the freezer to use whenever a recipe requires them.

Butter puff pastry
Use a puff pastry made with butter rather than margarine or other commercial fats. It's a little harder to work with as it's softer, so keep it refrigerated until you're ready to use it. Carême brand is an excellent choice.

Fish sauce
Megachef is a very good brand of fish sauce. Made in Thailand, it has a much gentler flavour than other brands.

Microherbs
Chefs use microherbs and microcress to add colour and flavour to dishes. They're available in punnets at some greengrocers and online. Snip off the leaves, being careful to avoid the soil in which they're growing, cover the remainder of the punnet loosely with a damp cloth and store in the fridge for up to a week; if unavailable, use the smallest leaves on a bunch of herbs.

Oyster sauce
Megachef is a reliable brand of oyster sauce naturally made in Thailand.

Paprika
The type of Spanish paprika you use will greatly affect the taste of a dish. The peppers used for paprika are either sundried or dried over a smoking fire, which imparts a distinctive flavour. Both unsmoked and smoked Spanish paprika come in three varieties: sweet (*dulce*), hot (*picante*) and sweet–sour (*agre dulce*); La Chinata is a good brand.

Preserved tuna
Spanish brand Ortiz makes excellent preserved tuna.

Tarragon
French tarragon is worth seeking out, as it has a vastly superior flavour to Russian tarragon; if French tarragon is unavailable, many chefs choose to use chervil instead, or simply leave it out.

Vinegar
Splash out on a good-quality wine vinegar and you'll notice the difference. Forum Cabernet Sauvignon and Chardonnay vinegars are very good, as are those made by Australian company LiraH.

ACKNOWLEDGEMENTS

A cookbook takes a lot of time to create – time that would otherwise be spent with family and friends and on other projects. So thanks first of all to my ever-supportive husband, Franz Scheurer, and to my close family and friends for understanding why I can't 'come out to play' as often as I'd like to!

Huge thanks to my incredible team at Sydney Seafood School, who keep things running so smoothly whether I'm there or not: my right and left hands in the office, Fiona Forsyth and Elizabeth Patchett; in the School, our demonstrators Brigid Treloar, Coralie Riordan and Julie Ray; assistants Fiona Baxter, Jen Vickery, Vincenza Scalone, Vicky Wilhelmus, Lara Reynolds, Jeff Chandler and Jason Ray; and kitchenhands Vinod Bassi and Gerard Riordan.

Many thanks also to Fiona B, Jen, Vicky, Vincenza and Lara for their help with recipe testing and preparing food for the book's photography and Vincenza also for her work on the step-by-step photos. Thanks to Gus Dannoun and Mark Boulter for checking species information.

My deep gratitude to Sydney Fish Market Managing Director, Grahame Turk, who has always been so supportive of me and the School, and without whom this book would not have come into being.

The chefs who teach at the School are the embodiment of 'hospitality'. They give their time, energy and knowledge so generously – they are what makes this industry such a joy to work in. Thanks to all our wonderful guest chefs and presenters, and especially to the 49 chefs whose recipes are in this book. I appreciate your patience and input more than I can say. Thank you for sharing your recipes and stories, for always being there to answer 'just one more question', for your help with preparing and plating food, and for making yourselves available for the photoshoot.

Thanks to all our suppliers – especially Wayne from Joto, who tied himself in knots to get everything we needed for the photoshoot, and Christie's, who were always on hand and happy to help when we needed something 'now!'

Last – but by no means least – thanks to Publisher Julie Gibbs and her band of Penguins, who make writing a book such a wonderful experience. Thanks Julie for embracing this project, Ariane Durkin for your diligent editing, Arielle Gamble for your beautiful design, Alan Benson for the gorgeous photographs, Clio Kempster for arranging the photoshoot so smoothly and Sarah O'Brien for props and styling.

INDEX

LANTERN

Published by the Penguin Group
Penguin Group (Australia)
707 Collins Street, Melbourne, Victoria 3008, Australia
(a division of Pearson Australia Group Pty Ltd)
Penguin Group (USA) Inc.
375 Hudson Street, New York, New York 10014, USA
Penguin Group (Canada)
90 Eglinton Avenue East, Suite 700, Toronto, Canada ON M4P 2Y3
(a division of Pearson Penguin Canada Inc.)
Penguin Books Ltd
80 Strand, London WC2R 0RL England
Penguin Ireland
25 St Stephen's Green, Dublin 2, Ireland
(a division of Penguin Books Ltd)
Penguin Books India Pvt Ltd
11 Community Centre, Panchsheel Park, New Delhi – 110 017, India
Penguin Group (NZ)
67 Apollo Drive, Rosedale, North Shore 0632, New Zealand
(a division of Pearson New Zealand Ltd)
Penguin Books (South Africa) (Pty) Ltd
Rosebank Office Park, Block D, 181 Jan Smuts Avenue, Parktown North,
Johannesburg 2196, South Africa

Penguin Books Ltd, Registered Offices: 80 Strand, London, WC2R 0RL, England

First published by Penguin Group (Australia), 2012

10 9 8 7 6 5 4 3 2

Design by Arielle Gamble © Penguin Group (Australia)

Illustrations by Arielle Gamble and Iona Fraser
Original blackboard ID concept by Michael McCann (dreamtime australia
design), and Wallcandy

Author photograph by Alan Benson
Props styling by Sarah O'Brien

Typeset in Livory & Scala Sans by Post Pre-Press Group, Brisbane, Queensland
Printed and bound in China by 1010 Printing International Ltd

National Library of Australia
Cataloguing-in-Publication entry:

    Muir, Roberta, 1962–

    Sydney Seafood School cookbook /Roberta Muir, author;
    Alan Benson, photographer

    9781921382765 (hbk.)

    Includes index.

    Sydney Seafood School.

    Cooking (Seafood)--New South Wales--Sydney.

    641.692

penguin.com.au/lantern

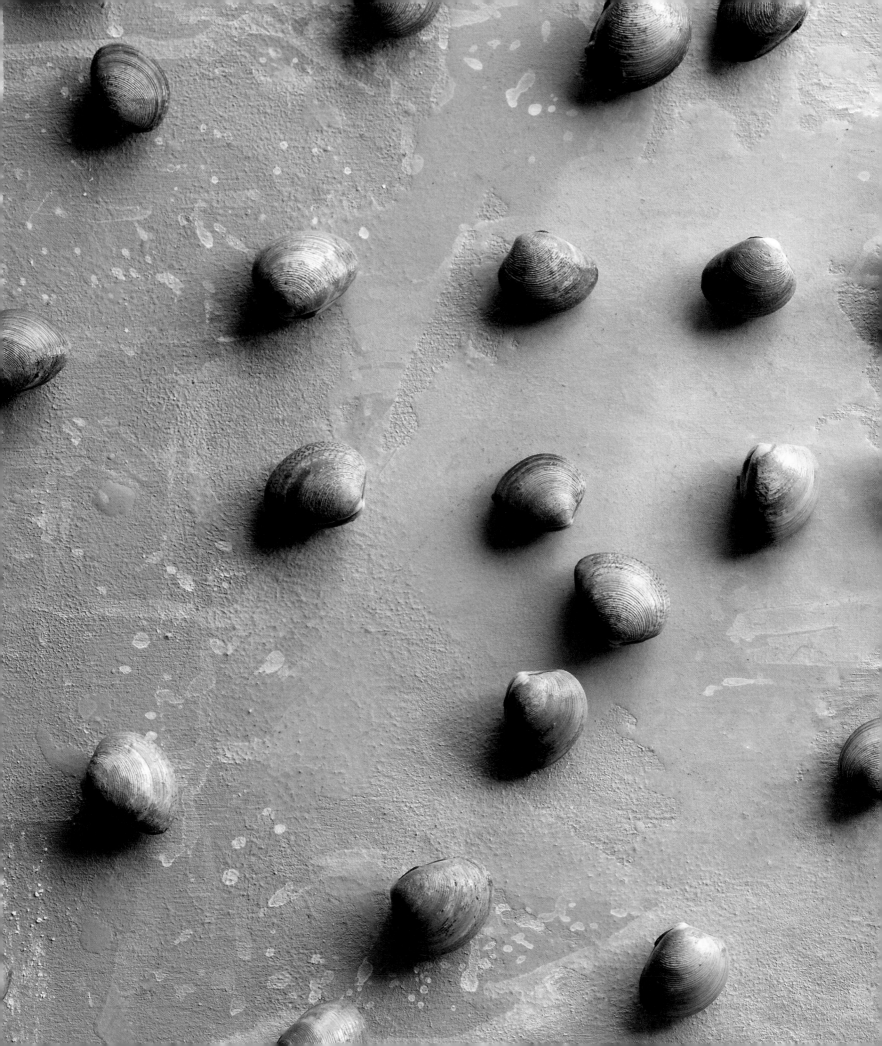

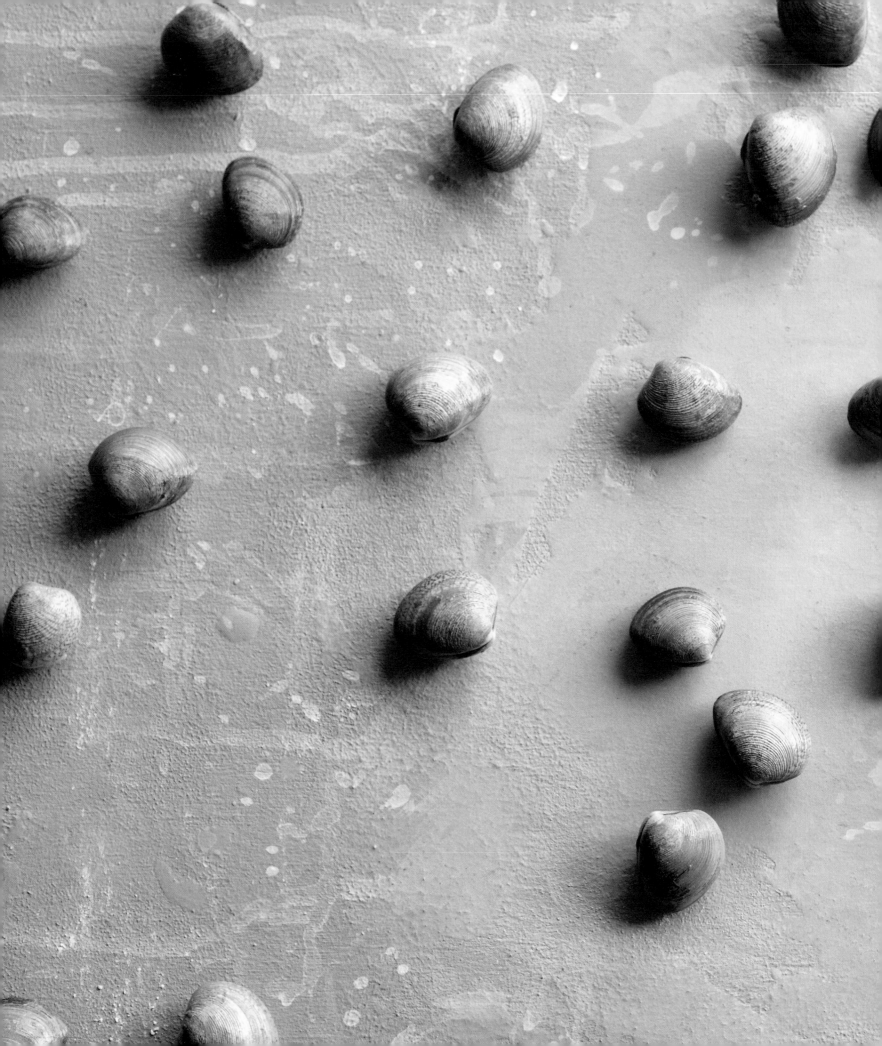